JUNE 2 B'DAY
PABLO

DEATH SENTENCES

How Clichés, Weasel Words, and Management-Speak are Strangling Public Language

•

DON WATSON

GOTHAM
BOOKS

GOTHAM BOOKS
Published by Penguin Group (USA) Inc.
375 Hudson Street, New York, New York 10014, U.S.A.

Penguin Group (Canada), 90 Eglinton Avenue East, Suite 700, Toronto, Ontario, Canada
M4P 2Y3 (a division of Pearson Penguin Canada Inc.); Penguin Books Ltd, 80 Strand,
London WC2R 0RL, England; Penguin Ireland, 25 St Stephen's Green, Dublin 2,
Ireland (a division of Penguin Books Ltd); Penguin Group (Australia),
250 Camberwell Road, Camberwell, Victoria 3124, Australia (a division of
Pearson Australia Group Pty Ltd); Penguin Books India Pvt Ltd, 11 Community Centre,
Panchsheel Park, New Delhi - 110 017, India; Penguin Group (NZ), cnr Airborne and
Rosedale Roads, Albany, Auckland 1310, New Zealand (a division of Pearson
New Zealand Ltd); Penguin Books (South Africa) (Pty) Ltd, 24 Sturdee Avenue,
Rosebank, Johannesburg 2196, South Africa

Penguin Books Ltd, Registered Offices: 80 Strand, London WC2R 0RL, England

Published by Gotham Books, a division of Penguin Group (USA) Inc.

First published in Australia by Knopf in 2003.
Published as *Gobbledygook* in the UK by Atlantic Books.
Published as a Gotham Books hardcover edition in 2005.

First trade paperback printing, May 2006

10 9 8 7 6 5 4 3 2 1

Gotham Books and the skyscraper logo are trademarks of Penguin Group (USA) Inc.

The Library of Congress has catalogued the hardcover edition of this title as follows:
Watson, Don, 1949–
Death sentences : how clichés, weasel words and management-speak are strangling
public language / Don Watson.
        p.   cm.
Includes bibliographical references (p.).
ISBN 1-592-40140-6 (hardcover)
ISBN 1-592-40205-4 (paperback)
1. English language—Errors of usage.   2. Cliché—English-speaking countries.
3. English language—Terms and phrases.   4. English language—Jargon.
5. Management—Terminology.   6. Jargon (Terminology)   1. Title.
PE1460.W325 2005
428—dc22   2004060879

Printed in the United States of America
Set in Garamond 3 with Serlio

CONTENTS

•

·

Preface
to the U.S. Edition

Don Watson is one of Australia's best-known writers and public intellectuals. For more than twenty-five years he has written books, essays and reviews for the stage and television. He was for part of his life a political satirist and for another part a political speechwriter, including four years with Paul Keating, the former Labor Prime Minister. His 2001 *Recollections of a Bleeding Heart: A Portrait of Paul Keating PM* was a #1 national bestseller and a multiple award winner. He lives and works in Melbourne and lectures widely on writing and language.

Praise for *Death Sentences*:

"Watson makes an eloquent, elegant, and sometimes scathing case for taking back language from those who would strip it of all color and emotion and, therefore, of all meaning. . . . With admirable clarity and logic, Watson makes the decay of language an issue of prime importance for everyone, not just wordsmiths."
—Joanne Wilkinson, *Booklist*

". . . many lessons and insights in this book. . . ."
—Leigh Buchanan, *Harvard Business Review*

"[Watson's] always clear and precise, even when exposing the verbal pollution that passes for wisdom in the public realm." —Ellen Roseman, *Toronto Star*

"[Watson] captures the powerlessness and frustration we feel when confronted by meaningless words delivered with authority." —*Los Angeles Times Book Review*

"As Don Watson's smart and funny book demonstrates, mind-numbing obfuscation is spreading. The book is full of sentences that crackle with energy. Watson wields the language like a bullwhip."
—John Wilkens, *The San Diego Union-Tribune*

"It is a brilliant book. . . . Anyone who has been forced to compose a 'mission statement' knows exactly what I mean."
—Bill Ruehlmann, *The Virginian-Pilot*

THIS BOOK WAS NOT WRITTEN BY A LINGUIST ON BEHALF of the language, or by a grammarian on behalf of grammar. I am not qualified for either of those enterprises. The book is written from my experience as a writer and a reader and, if it is written on behalf of anyone, it is the people who have to write and read and listen to our public language every day of their lives. It is an argument on behalf of what these days are called the stakeholders. For four years, I was the Australian prime minister's speechwriter, and for four years before that I combined writing speeches for a state premier with writing political satire for a comedian. I wrote on history and politics in the newspapers. Now and then, I wrote speeches for corporate chief executives. I wrote—or rewrote—company brochures and in-house training manuals. I gave occasional seminars on writing for government departments, corporate communications teams, and conferences of schoolteachers. In all these places I came across language that was all but dead and people who seemed willing to join in its destruction. Over fifteen years, I saw the plague accelerate and spread from the private to the public realms, from the global to the local, to churches and to schools where, at eleven years of age, my granddaughter was required to prepare her very own personal mission statement, and at age twelve wrote her first English essay in PowerPoint. My grievance, I confess, is personal.

The earliest symptoms of what became my permanent gripe showed up in the last half of the 1980s when I was working for a premier. It was then I found I could not understand the information sent me by government officials for turning into speeches. I wondered if the job required a better mind than mine to grasp the concepts underlying politics and public policy. But it was the language of those public servants' briefs: It worked on me like too much Valium. One paragraph and my mind swam, consciousness drifted. Whatever thoughts the words contained, I could not reach them: I could not understand because I could not make myself interested.

Around the same time, while moonlighting with a multinational chemical company, I came across Total Quality Management (TQM). I was curious about TQM and I believed the people who told me about the wonders it worked in companies. But when asked to write it in attractive or plain English I did not know how. I could not distinguish the thoughts from the phrases in which they came. As one cannot separate cement from cement, one cannot say "a structured system for satisfying internal and external customers and suppliers by integrating the business environment, continuous improvement, and breakthroughs with development, improvement, and maintenance cycles while changing organizational culture" without saying "structured system," "satisfying internal and external customers," "integrating the business environment," "continuous improvement," and so on. In this language the only thing left to a writer is to shuffle the phrases and experiment with verbs. So you will see, for instance, that in its mission statement the guided missile manufacturer BAE Systems prefers *delighting* its customers to *satisfying* them.

In time, I learned that this was the beauty of management jargon, the unbreakable code. Anyone could write it and, with a little practice, speak it, and just to write or speak the stuff was to prove you were professional: so professional that every underling who could not crack the code must imitate you. The miracle was that once you knew a dozen or so "key" or "core" terms, once you were "focused" on them, thought was scarcely necessary. In fact, writing like this was best done, and perhaps could *only* be done, without thinking at all.

I took the job with the prime minister, and in his office became aware that the now customer-focused and service-driven federal bureaucracy had added TQM and other management jargon to their own traditionally plentiful store. It was in these years that my grievance became a small obsession. I came to loathe "enhanced," "vibrant," and "commitment," to name just three. It was like getting fleas off a dog, but in the end the prime minister's office was cleansed. No one used "enhanced," "vibrant," or "commitment"; they were forbidden, abolished.

All resistance was in vain, of course. The Information Revolution came in on top of the Management Revolution. The Technological Revolution tumbled in with both of them. Economies were global. Markets were free, at least ideologically speaking. The unstoppable tide washed into all the corners of our lives. The local library got a mission statement; the church called its mission to the poor "excellence in hospitality"; the kindergarten became outcomes-based; and, entering into the spirit of marketing and focus groups, politics turned "values-based" and worked primarily in messages. Much that we used to call society became the economy and, being an *information* economy, language was drafted to its service. Everywhere—public and private, all levels of government and all government agencies, the military, schools, health, politics, media—the language was co-opted, hacked about, gutted. Worlds of meaning—the cultural equivalent of many lakes, rain forests, and species—disappeared. And hardly a voice was heard protesting.

When this book was published in Australia, no one, including its author, expected it to sell many more than the first print run of five thousand copies. That was almost two years ago, when it was well known that books about language sold only to specialists and pedants. Now we know otherwise. The fashion may not last as long as books about celebrities or terrorism, but just now it is possible for books about language to become number-one bestsellers. Tens of thousands of people buy them; and it seems that for each ten thousand, two hundred or so are inspired to write letters to the author, and of those a dozen or so invite him to speak at a conference or give a lecture of some kind. Books about language now oblige their authors to hire assistants and start Web sites. They get them thinking about writing sequels. There can only be one reason for this gratifying clamor: Far more people than we thought cherish the language, and the evidence of its decay dismays them.

A year and a half after the book was published in Australia, the letters still arrive. They come from people obliged to use management language in their jobs with big corporations, small companies, and all kinds of government departments, including departments of education; from teachers who are compelled to instruct children in language none of them understands; from people who, by some Orwellian fiat, have become "customers" and "stakeholders"— even "valued" customers and "valued" stakeholders—and cannot stand it anymore. They come from people who hear something sinister in the anesthetizing jargon of management and politics, and from people who read it as a symptom of decline in culture, morality, and democracy.

Some of the letters are anecdotal, and some recommend to me the writings of Karl Kraus, who believed the abuse of language was a moral crime; or of Martin Heidegger, who believed that "our being is founded in language." Heidegger's point is that our being cannot be founded in modern technical or "calculative" language, or the kind that aims at "uniform accessibility of everything to everyone." This is a fair description of contemporary public language, and when he insists that such language undermines aesthetics, morality, and being, Heidegger might be trying to make the same point in theory that many of my correspondents make with their stories from experience. I mean people such as those who say they worked for years in jobs concerned with "communications" without ever quite understanding what they were doing. The teachers who can no longer write students' reports, but instead must tick the box next to the "calculative," "outcomes-based" description that they guess comes closest to their own assessment of each child's progress—or rather the child's "essential learnings and key competencies." ("Outcomes," by the way, "describe what students learn about and what they do, as a result of the teaching and learning in the course.") Or the man who said that on the day he had to leave his old father in a nursing home, the most difficult thing to bear was not the parting or the three-hour wait in the foyer, but the mission statement on the wall: the sign proclaiming, WE WILL EXCEED ALL YOUR EXPECTATIONS. It drove him mad then, and it still drives him mad.

Some of these reports from the front line are sad, despairing letters; others are ironic and derisive. There are letters from schoolchildren and from people who have been "downsized" or "rightsized" or "structurally adjusted." A few write thinking they have recognized a fellow curmudgeon. I expected more of these, and more from folk wanting to correct my grammar. What I did not expect was so much gratitude. Never did a writer feel more appreciated. They tell me that they now feel less alone, that they had for so long thought they were the only ones, in the government department, on the bank's communications team, at the human resources conference, in the school staff room, or on the board of the library who could not understand what their colleagues were saying—and whatever they did make of it sounded like baloney.

Today someone writes to say that while proofreading the annual report of a large welfare agency he came upon this sentence: "The ensuing months saw the creative development of a comprehensive suite of collateral including envelopes, business cards, letterheads, and design templates." It is not the punctuation or the grammar that concerns him, but rather the stationery described as a "comprehensive suite of collateral," the "ensuing months" (they "ensued" from a "branding conference"), the "creative" element. It's the pomposity of the thing, the loss of proportion, the folly of it. My correspondent wrote in the margin of the document, "What does this mean?" A manager sent it back with a note attached: "It's corporate language." He was not offering an apology or an excuse, but a justification, as if "corporate language" were a requirement of incorporation, or as if it fulfilled a duty as doctors once thought it did to write prescriptions in Latin.

Lawyers might make a more instructive comparison. Law used to be the foundation of public language, but now management is. Legal language can be arcane, obscure, and pompous, but management language is much worse. There is a provenance to law that management lacks, and it is capable of elegance and force. The lawyer Abraham Lincoln will do for evidence of this. Legal language at least has its roots in the same ground as the language the rest of us speak. But management language is newfangled in root and branch and rarely sounds like anything but hokum.

It is thus well suited to politics and the media and to what Eric Alterman last year called in the *Nation* the "post-truth political environment." Management-speak is a great gap-filler. It is hollow, pompous, and modern in just the right proportions. Its leaden phrases makes the vapid sound concrete, and obscures the thoughts that inspired them from listener and speaker, reader and writer alike. There is no better instrument than management jargon to soften us up for the "non-truth political environment."

If we get used to business calling every little change a new paradigm or a paradigm shift, we might not be as frightened as we should be when presidents announce that the world's greatest democracy is now governed by a new paradigm. When "enhanced" has been exhausted of all meaning by a decade of overuse, we might be less inclined to wonder what is meant by "enhanced interrogation techniques." When we are accustomed to corporations of all kinds telling us they are dedicated equally to delighting their clients and being "values-based," who will smell hypocrisy or danger when politicians tell us that they are too? If we believe the words of mission statements, or don't believe them but see the point, what won't we believe or see the point in? When the everyday words of the workplace are hollow and stripped of meaning, it is certain that they will become the words used in politics. That is the deepest concern. Of course, one is for the language: for plainness and elegance and genius, especially the genius of the vernacular. But one is equally for the democracy and the quality of mind that language serves and expresses, and upon which it depends.

·

INTRODUCTION

•

"Third generation strategy maps have been designed to overcome the limitations that have made balanced score-cards notoriously difficult to fully implement. . . . The strategy map begins with a strategic goal, is followed immediately with a strategic value proposition and ends with a cause and effect systems diagram that outlines what needs to be done to achieve results."
    —OREGON HEALTH AND SCIENCE UNIVERSITY

•

"Base words are uttered only by the base
And can for such at once be understood,
But noble platitudes:—ah, there's a case
Where the most careful scrutiny is needed
To tell a voice that's genuinely good
From one that's base but merely has succeeded."
    —W. H. AUDEN, "SHORTS," *COLLECTED SHORTER POEMS 1930–1934*

•

"A great ox stands on my tongue."
    —AESCHYLUS

•

PUBLIC LANGUAGE CONFRONTS MOST OF US EVERY DAY of our lives, but rarely when we are with friends or family. Not yet, at least. It is not the language in which we address lovers, postmen, children, or pets. So far.

True, in the households of young professionals they will say sometimes that the new dog *adds alpha to their lifestyle;* that they need *closure* with their orthodontist or mother; that they are *empowered* by their Nikes. There is seepage from the public to the private. But that's all it is. *At this point in time.* We hope.

But it may be worse than it seems, much worse. What if the irritation or dejection we feel upon hearing the U.S. president speak or receiving a letter from a bank or a government department were symptoms of permanent and accelerating decline? Martin Amis might be right. "The professionalization of ordinary existence: this is the enemy within." Language, after all, defines ordinary existence. "Speak, that I may see thee." It's how we know each other.

Public language is the language of public life: the language of political and business leaders and civil servants—official, formal, sometimes elevated language. It is the language of leaders more than the led, managers rather than the managed. It takes very different forms: from shapely rhetoric to shapeless, enervating sludge; but in every case, for good or ill, it is the language of power and influence. What our duties are, for whom we should vote, which mobile phone plan we should take up: in all these places the public language rules.

As power and influence are pervasive, so is the language: we hear and read it at the highest levels and at the lowest. And while it begins with the powerful, the weak are often obliged to speak it: to recite it, imitate it and, in the information age, work with it. "Even politicians speak/truths of value to the weak," Auden said. Believing as they do that we all need something, even if we don't know it, marketing people would agree.

The influence of marketing shows itself in advertising and commerce, where we would expect to find it, and in politics and war, where its presence might surprise us. Marketing goes wherever the media go, and the media go pretty well everywhere, including war zones, which means wars require media management and marketing like everything else. *Embedded journalists,* or *embeds,* were borne of this requirement, and so were many words, including *attriting,* a new one for killing and maiming.

The same *professionalized* language comes to politics because increasing numbers of politicians are *professionals.* Many have management and marketing training and experience behind them. In Donald Rumsfeld one can even hear clear traces of Est, the seminal Californian variety of Large

Group Awareness Training. Est made popular the word *closure*, and the concept—or craze—of *self-actualization.* It spread the word of Human Potential, which created vast, luxurious fields for the consultancy industry. Est's mixture of Zen, Scientology, Dianetics, Maslow, gestalt, Napoleon Hill, and Dale Carnegie had a significant influence on the strand of management that murders language more efficiently than any other, Human Resources (HR).

By adopting HR and its various associated creeds, including Knowledge Management and Neurolinguistic Programming, educational institutions and other organizations created to provide enlightenment, assistance, and care speak a language that dulls the senses and cannot express sentiment. A dead language. Thus public education takes on the same management and accounting principles as private companies created to make profits. They take on the same consultants, and consultants, many of them *downsized* from useful vocations, are the plague rats of the language virus.

•

All kinds of institutions now cannot tell us about their services, including the most piddling change in them, without also telling us that they are *contemporary, innovative and forward-looking,* and *committed to continuous improvement,* as if the decision to raise their rates or change their phone number can be grasped only in this *context-sensitive* way. To help us all get going in the same direction they might give the context a name, like *Growing Together* or *Business Line Plus,* or *Operation Decapitation* when the service is a military one.

Managerialism, a name for various doctrines of business organization, also comes with a language of its own, and to such unlikely places as political parties and educational institutions. Even if the organizational principles of management or marketing were so widely appropriate, in most cases their language is not. Marketing, for instance, has no particular concern with truth. Management concerns are relatively narrow—relative, that is, to life, knowledge, and possibility. This alone makes marketing and managerial language less than ideal for a democracy or a college. In addition, such language lacks almost everything needed to put into words an opinion or an emotion; to explain the complex, paradoxical, or uncertain; to tell a joke. If those who propagate this blather really believed in being *context-sensitive,* they would understand that in the context of ordinary human needs and sensibility their language is extraordinarily *in*sensitive. It enrages, depresses, humiliates, confuses. It leaves us speechless.

Public language that defies normal understanding is, as Primo Levi wrote, "an ancient repressive artifice, known to all churches, the typical vice of our political class, the foundation of all colonial empires." The politicians, the managers, the consultants, the facilitators, the economists will tell you it is in the interests of leadership, management, efficiency, *stakeholders,* the *bottom line,* or some organizational imperative, but the public language is, in essence, the language of power. It has its origins in the subjection or control of one person by another. In all societies, "to take power is to win speech."

It will not always be obvious, of course, but intimidation and manipulation come as naturally to public language as polite instruction and enlightenment. Lies and distortion also come naturally, even among the well-intentioned. The complex is rendered simple, the simple complex. Sordid and self-interested deeds become examples of selfless heroism; true heroes are overlooked or airbrushed out. Cynics and pragmatists are made into people of high purpose, people prepared to make *hard decisions*. Myth, legends, fantasies, and lies are the traditional stuff of public language. That is why vigilance is needed: an argument concerning the public language is an argument concerning liberty.

•

To Levi's list of obfuscating types we could add many sociologists and deconstructionists, including some who design school curricula and courses with the word "studies" in them. For blighting the world with years of pious variations on *access and equity, gender equity, rich multicultural diversity,* and other clichés of the left, political correctness has a case to answer. When the politically correct meets the managerial—usually in civil service departments—horrors are born in the language. People are likely to establish an *EOWA Women in Management Tools Module 5,* and go about saying that *Increased energy for improving employment outcomes for women can be obtained by engaging a broad range of men as EO partners;* that what they need most is *quality participation opportunities and sustainability;* that they must *implement and achieve enhanced values;* and that *a focus on outcome targets without an emphasis on improved employment practices will not deliver support from men and will not result in sustainable changes to improve gender equity outcomes.*

But the politically correct do not deserve all the blame. Eight years ago, the Australian prime minister, John Howard, came to office denouncing political correctness and encouraging free expression among those who had, he said, been silenced by left-wing "thought police." Disaffected xenophobes and racists took advantage of the offer, and Australian politics turned sharply to the right. Critics of government policy were labeled *elites, chattering classes,* and—most devastating of all—*latte drinkers.* After a few years John Howard declared his mission accomplished: good citizens who had been cowed by these urban elites were now saying what was on their minds, he said. Mr. Howard had liberated his people from political correctness, or at least from the left-wing version of it. But he had not liberated the language. The language is much worse than it was when he started.

Political correctness and its equally irritating twin, anti-political correctness; economic rationalism; dope smoking; Knowledge Management—wherever fashion and cults exist, the language inclines to the arcane or inscrutable. This is no bad thing in itself, but obnoxious in a democratic or educational environment. Among Druids, Masons, or economists we expect the language to be unfathomable or at least unclear or strange. They speak in code. This can only be because they do not want us to understand, or do not themselves understand, or are so in the habit of speaking this way they have lost the ability to communicate normally. When we hear this sort of language, it is, therefore, common sense to assume there is a cult, or something like a cult, in the vicinity. And what if everywhere we read and hear people saying: *The team, whether or not it is acceptant of the change, now puts itself on the curve . . .* Or, *identify major change drivers impacting on the sectors . . . ; enterprise and sector strategies to address the impact of the strategies.* Or, *penetration, development and expansion of the vertical market segment and strategic close of high impact deals?* We must assume that the cult has taken over.

While English spreads across the globe, the language

itself is shrinking. Vast numbers of new words enter it every year, but both our children's and our leaders' vocabularies are getting smaller. Latin and Greek have been squeezed out of most journalists' English, and "obscure" words are forbidden unless they qualify as economic or business jargon. You write for your audience, and your audience knows fewer words than it used to and hasn't time to look up unfamiliar ones. The language of politics is tuned to the same audience and uses the same media to reach it, so it too diminishes year by year. *Downsized,* business would say. Business language is a desert. Like a public company, the public language is being trimmed of excess and subtlety; what it doesn't need is shed, what is useful is reorganized, *prioritized,* and attached either to new words or to old ones stripped of meaning. In business, language is now *productivity-driven.*

What of the media, whose words we read and hear every day? The code of conduct of the International Federation of Journalists is categorical: "Respect for the truth and the right of the public to truth is the first duty of the journalist." There can be no respect for the truth without respect for the language. Only when language is alive does truth have a chance. As the powerful in legend turn the weak or the vanquished into stone, they turn us to stone through language. This is the function of a cliché, and of cant and jargon—to neutralize expression and "vanish memory." They are dead words. They will not do for truth.

Therefore, to live according to their code, journalists must choose their own words carefully and skillfully and insist that others do the same. The proper relationship of journalists to the public language is that of unrelenting critics. It is their duty to see through it. But we cannot rely on them. Norman Mailer once wrote on behalf of writers like himself that "the average reporter could not get a sentence straight if it were phrased more subtly than his own mind could make phrases." They munched nuances "like peanuts," he said. True, it happens and it's maddening, but weak prose is still journalism and roughly meets the requirements of the code. It is something else, however, when journalists ignore abuses of the public language by people of influence and power and reproduce without comment words that are intended to deceive and manipulate. When this happens, journalism ceases to be journalism and becomes a kind of propaganda, or a reflection of what Simone Weil called "the superb indifference that the powerful have for the weak."

The war in Iraq provided a case in point. The military provided brand names—*shock and awe,* for instance—and much of the media could see nothing but to use them. Each day of the campaign the media were briefed in the language of the Pentagon's media relations people, whereupon very often the journalists briefed their audiences in the same language. The media center in Doha was always *on message,* and so were the media. When the military said they had *degraded* by 70 percent a body of Iraqi soldiers, this was what the media reported. Few said "killed," and only the Iraqi minister for information in his daily self-satire said "slaughtered," which was a more honest word but a blatant lie because he said it of American soldiers, not Iraqi ones. One journalist, who knew something about the effects of Daisy Cutter bombs, said "puréed." And no one showed any pictures of the bodies. To be *embedded* with the coalition forces, or to be an *embed,* was to be *embedded* in their language and their *message.* It turned out that *embedded* just meant "in bed with" in the old language. If they said they had *attrited* an enemy force, generally that was what the media said, and it was the same if they said *deconflicted*.

All this was a sad retreat from both the journalists' code of conduct and the noble achievements of twentieth-century war reporting. Just as significant was the way these words spoke for the willingness of journalists to join the military in denying the common humanity of ordinary soldiers—especially the largely conscripted cannon fodder—on the opposing side. Here was another retreat: from war-reporting standards going back to Homer.

The public language will lift in tone and clarity only when those who write and speak it take words seriously again. They need to tune their ears to it. Awareness is the only defense against the creeping plague of which this is a microscopic specimen. *The inquiry may allow for relevant businesses or industries to be identified and for investigation into the possibility that certain regional or rural areas of the state would be more affected than others.* No doubt in the place from which these words came they were judged competent. But they are not competent in the world at large. They are not competent as language. They are an example of what George Orwell described as anesthetic writing. You cannot read it without losing a degree of consciousness. You come to, and read it again, and still your brain will not reveal the meaning—will not even try. You are getting sleepy again. Read aloud, in a speech for instance, an audience hears the words as they might hear a plane passing overhead or a television in another room. We can easily make it sound less like a distant airplane by simply saying it as if we mean it: *The inquiry will decide which businesses are relevant and which parts of the state will be badly affected.* In fact, to guess at the intended meaning, it might come down to *the inquiry deciding which businesses and which parts of the state will be most affected*. It's just one sentence. But we have to begin somewhere.

•

We must keep things in perspective, of course. The decay of language is not in itself life-threatening. It can be an aid to crime and tragedy; it can give us the reasons for unreasoning behavior, including war and genocide and even famine. Words are deadly. Words are bullets. But a word is not a weapon of mass destruction, or a jihad, or unhappiness. Like a rock, it is not a weapon (or a grinding stone) until someone picks it up and uses it as one. We should be careful not to sound too cranky or obsessive about words. You can't eat them or buy things with them, or protect your borders with them, and it will not do to make an exaggerated display of our concern. Make too much of a fuss and you will be quickly told that worse things are happening in the world than the decay of public language, that the *bottom line* is that language is not a *core issue*.

You might also be told that you are a kind of Luddite and must learn that resistance is futile! And a Luddite you are, to the extent that you cannot suffer language pressed into service by the information economy; language becoming to our times what steam engines and belts and pulleys were to the industrial age; language as an assembly line, an information implementer. It is full of *change drivers, core values, strategic implementation,* and *continuous improvement going forward*. It has no provenance and no memory. Like a machine or an assembly line, it removes the need for thinking: the uniquely human faculty of thought is suspended along with all sense of what feeling, need, or notion inspires your activity. Like assembly lines, this language is insensitive to human needs, including the need to have some control over what one is doing. People who are compelled to write and speak it every day will tell you they are never certain they know what the task is, or what the point of it is. The language seems designed to screen them from the meaning of their work, so they are never quite sure they know what they are trying to say or what is being said to them. Managerial language is an abuse of human rights. It robs people of their senses, their culture, and their tongue.

To the extent that it is molded and constrained by opinion polls, marketing and media spin, and infused with much of the same organizational doctrine, political language is the cousin of managerial language and just as alienating. To speak or be spoken to in either variety is to be "not in this world." It is to deal in a dead language. Ten years ago, when she received her Nobel Prize, the American novelist Toni Morrison described it this way:

> . . . a dead language is not only one no longer spoken or written, it is unyielding language content to admire its own paralysis. Like Statist language, censored and censoring. Ruthless in its policing duties, it has no desire or purpose other than maintaining the free range of its own narcotic narcissism, its own exclusivity and dominance. However moribund, it is not without effect for it actively thwarts the intellect, stalls conscience, suppresses human potential. Unreceptive to interrogation, it cannot form or tolerate new ideas, shape other thoughts, tell another story, fill baffling silences. Official language smitheryed to sanction ignorance and preserve privilege is a suit of

armor polished to shocking glitter, a husk from which
the knight departed long ago. Yet there it is: dumb,
predatory, sentimental. Exciting reverence in schoolchildren, providing shelter for despots, summoning false
memories of stability, harmony among the public.

If I deface a war memorial or rampage through St. Paul's
with a sledgehammer I will be locked up as a criminal or
lunatic. I can expect the same treatment if I release some
noxious weed or insect into the natural environment. It is
right that the culture and environment should be so re-
spected. Yet every day our leaders vandalize the language,
which is the foundation, the frame, and joinery of the culture, if not its greatest glory, and there is no penalty and no
way to impose one. We can only be indignant. And we
should resist.

•

CHAPTER 1

The Dark and Impenetrable Thicket

•

"We have got to exert ourselves a little to keep sane and call things by the names other people call them by."
—GEORGE ELIOT, *MIDDLEMARCH*

•

"The Park Lock cable on your tractor may not be adjusted properly resulting in park not engaging after the transmission shift level is moved to the 'park' position. As a result, unexpected nonpowered tractor movement may occur."
—JOHN DEERE SAFETY NOTICE

•

"In fact, the 'information needs identifier' should study, prepare, and equip him/herself thoroughly to perform the task of identifying information needs. . . . It is to be noted that methodology will become clearer and clearer as each step is put into practice enhancing the understanding of the scenario and help in fine tuning the procedure to suit particular situations,"
—PAPER PRESENTED TO A CONGRESS OF LIBRARIANS

•

"Toby's Individual Student Profile shows that he is achieving all the key indicators of Phase B on the Writing Developmental Continuum. He is also mapped as achieving Writing key indicators C1, C2, C3, C4 and C5. Although Toby is not yet operating in Phase C, he will not need to undertake the Writing validation task because he is already achieving both C2 and C5, which are part of the validation subset of indicators for Writing."
—SAMPLE STUDENT REPORT, QUEENSLAND

•

"Some children are not getting onto a growth trajectory as early as they should in terms of literacy."
—CHAIR OF THE AUSTRALIAN NATIONAL LITERACY REVIEW

PARROTS, WHEN THEY ARE SEPARATED FROM THEIR flocks, know by instinct that they must quickly join another one or they will make a meal for hawks. It is from this understanding that their mimetic skill derives. On finding any other horde, they try to blend in by mimicking its members. They do as the Romans do in flocks, or in families of humans. If it is a Catholic household in which they find themselves, they might recite Hail Marys. Among blasphemers, they'll blaspheme. Where it is customary to curse the dog or tap the barometer, they curse the dog or tap the barometer. Whatever is most frequently repeated sounds to them definitive, and this is what they imitate. Every day for forty years, regardless of the context, a bird might screech "Don't forget your hat!" or shout "Oh, What a Feeling!" all day long, much as advertisers do. Parrots never learn the language but are smart enough to know, like people involved in marketing, that one or two catchphrases will satisfy most people.

Our language grows, mutates, and ossifies in a similar way. We are all inclined to imitate the sounds we hear. Fashion dictates many words and phrases. In foreign countries we pick up accents and inflections. We tune ourselves to the cadences of unfamiliar dining rooms. Politicians go among the people, primed with local knowledge, and saying "G'day" or "How do you do," according to the prevailing custom. Priests murmur Latin phrases that are full of meaning even to their non–Latin-speaking flocks. Street gangs, sports clubs, political parties, families, and people who for all kinds of reasons are regularly together naturally develop a vernacular as a means of bonding, and those who wish to join must learn it. Ideologues speak in language best understood by ideologues of like mind: it is called "preaching to the converted," and it is probably a species of narcissism, like a budgerigar talking to itself in a mirror.

Organizations frequently impose a language of a certain shape on members and employees. Military forces seem to have done it always, and now companies imitate the military example, and all kinds of other outfits imitate the companies. Politics took slogans from military battalions—the word "slogan" comes from the Gaelic and literally means "battle cry." No sooner were there slogans in politics than there were also "weasel words": sly expressions that do not mean what they appear to, or have an unseen purpose. To be involved with politics is to make a pact with the devil, Max Weber said. Should we then expect the language of politics to have something diabolical about it? And if politicians can't resist temptation, why should advertising and marketing? Why should companies? The company is a miracle of the modern world: in fact it is almost true to say that the limited-liability company was the beginning of the modern age. The point at which the age becomes *post*modern is marked, perhaps, by companies taking their liability for the language to be limited.

The English language has always been prey to fashion, and on the evidence so far we should not fear for its survival. Fashions come and go, and the language moves on, taking with it whatever remains useful or interesting, discarding what is colorless or vain. The language has proved much stronger than any human attempt to contain it: Samuel Johnson and, on the other side of the Atlantic, Noah Webster both tried to tie it down, and both failed magnificently. Waves of grammarians have followed them. There have always been people keen to declare that this or that is the only definition of a word, and this is the only way to pronounce it; this is the only way to arrange a sentence, and this the only way to punctuate it. These people are essential, but only in the way that lifeboats are to an ocean liner.

The historical view suggests we can relax. English has survived everything that's been thrown at it: political and social revolution, industrial and technological revolutions, colonialism and postcolonialism, mass education, mass media, mass society. More than just surviving these upheavals, it adapts and grows, is strengthened and enriched by them. And never has it grown more than now: by one estimate, at the rate of more than twenty thousand words per year, and for every new word several old ones disappear, change their meanings, or sprout additional ones. The adaptability is wondrous.

And yet as it grows, it is depleting and, in its center, may be dying. In the information age the public language is reducing to an ugly, subliterate universal form with a fraction of the richness that living English has. Relative to the potential of language, this new form approximates a parrot's usage. It is cliché-ridden and lacks meaning, energy, imagery, and rhythm. It also lacks words. It struggles to express the human. Buzzwords abound in it. Platitudes iron it flat. The language is hostile to communion, which is the purpose of language. It cannot touch provenance. It stifles reason, imagination, and the promise of truth. Look at a block of 1960s council flats and you have the shape and dysfunction of it. Listen and you can hear the echoes of authoritarian cant. Our public language is becoming a nonlanguage.

Errors of grammar are irritating; slovenly, colloquial, or hybrid speech can be gruesome; but English also gets much of its vigor and resilience from spontaneous invention and the colonial cultural mix. Compared to the general malaise, even the language of the law is harmless and at least amuses those who practice it. These failings are to the language as a few biting insects are to the tsetse fly: as an itch is to a slow, sleeping death.

•

Whereas earlier generations were inclined to quote from poets, the present one employs them. *Wordsmiths,* they call them. The Australian prime minister (and a minister in the government before his) engaged the poet Les Murray to write an Oath of Allegiance, a burst of rhetoric by which the people might forever know themselves. They engaged him less as a poet and more as a plumber. They employed him literally, prosaically. They never felt obliged to dip into his poems. He was just another consultant to be called on for his skills, or just as likely to add a bit of class that for ten times the price McKinsey's could not come up with. It is the last word in specialization, surely, when the country's unofficial poet laureate is treated as just another expert.

Implicit in the recruiting of *wordsmiths* to the political and corporate cause is the notion that writing is an activity distinct from thinking. In fact, every writer knows that it's in the writing that many ideas are formed. (This may be one reason why many brilliant writers are far from brilliant speakers.) Government and corporate powers go on thinking in what they imagine are the only ways for governments and corporations to think, and employ writers to tinker with the words. The next generation may not believe that there was a time when people in business and government were able to think *and* write at the same time.

In the modern public service, the career of John Maynard Keynes might have terminally stalled, not because he was a Keynesian in a non-Keynesian age but because he wrote in a style that intelligent laypeople understood and even enjoyed. It is even possible that had he written as they write nowadays he would not have been able to think his way to a Keynesian position. Something similar can be assumed of Lincoln's Gettysburg speech, which in the end is a poem. Peggy Noonan, Ronald Reagan's speechwriter, famously amended Gettysburg in the way a team of Washington advisers might have. Virtually nothing remained of the poetry or the substance—nothing, at least, to live beyond the next day's news. Today's advisers, well trained in quality management and perhaps even Neurolinguistic Programming, might turn Gettysburg into something like this:

Eighty-seven years ago our great-grandfathers and -grandmothers built a capacity for the implementation of a new nation [partnering God] with a commitment to harnessing synergies for enhanced outcomes for all stakeholders going forward. Today we are confronting the challenge of seeing whether hopefully a country with these commitments and these synergies will still be there at the end of the day.

This is nonsense, of course: no consultants worthy of the name would write a mission statement in whole sentences. They use PowerPoint. It is the only way to order thoughts and, with the software selling hundreds of millions of copies, no doubt the only way that some people can recognize them. Colin Powell used PowerPoint when he made the case for invading Iraq to the UN. It worked fine, if you ignore the errors of fact. Bullet points and slides have an appearance of truth that is largely illusory. For proof of this we need only look on the Internet for Peter Norvig's Satirical Gettysburg in PowerPoint. The format kills the words. It doesn't work. PowerPoint, as Edward R. Tufte of Harvard says, "allows speakers to pretend they are giving a real talk and audiences to pretend that they are listening." It is, he says, "a prankish conspiracy against substance and thought," and may even lead to a decline in cognitive abilities. Whatever the truth of that claim, we can be sure it is doing no good to the language. But PowerPoint continues to spread, from business to politics to increasing numbers of schools, where it is preferred in junior English to sentences and essays.

The difference between this and previous ages seems to be that in ours the same clichés find their way everywhere. No class or category of work or wealth confines them. They defy educational and occupational barriers. What you hear on daytime television you will also hear from an MP, from a chief executive, from a high school student. Not long ago the word "customers" was generally understood—with a few variations—to mean purchasers or clients, people who took their custom to a shop or some other kind of commercial establishment. Now libraries and universities and nursing homes have *customers* instead of readers, students, and patients. Taxation departments have customers instead of taxpayers or citizens, just as the CIA and McDonald's have *customers*. Do not be surprised if one day you hear an American general talk of *enemy customers*—of *attriting* them, quite possibly.

Flaubert's *Dictionary of Received Ideas* was a compendium of clichés, "idiotic" bourgeois terms, and social responses. No doubt it was clever when it was written, but now it is altogether too clever. A politician who used the clichés mocked by Flaubert would dazzle us with originality. Take the word "paradox." He writes: "always originates on the Boulevard des Italiens between two puffs on a cigarette." Very good indeed; but what we would give for a public figure to recognize a paradox, or a dilemma, or even a little ambiguity and invite us to share in the puzzle. Flaubert quotes the clichéd use of "gaiety" (always preceded by "frantic"). When did we last hear the word used? Is there a significant public figure we can even imagine using it? Or "felicity"? Or "Abelard"? Or "odalisk"? He says of the word "hard"—invariably "as iron." But no one says *hard as iron* anymore. They say *hard decisions,* which is to say uncomfortably difficult. A *hard decision* is closely related to *there are no quick fixes*, a tiresomely familiar expression that compounds the platitudinous with condescension.

Managerial language rarely evokes the physical world,

another reason there is no life in it. Where Flaubert heard nauseating condescension we might hear something genuine: *farm workers*—what would we do without them? There are now too few farm workers to be worth a politician's time. If, however, a politician said *What would we do without you?* to workers in a call center or some other modern workplace, he might move their hearts. The words would impress people who caught them on the evening news. Some viewers might even shed tears, because they are used to hearing people say *we value your contribution; we appreciate your commitment; you have our gratitude going forward*. After you've heard these words a hundred times, *What would we do without you?* sounds direct, heartfelt, human, generous.

Flaubert mocks it, but how much happier we would be if our bank said *a sword of Damocles* was hanging over us, or that we were in a *dark and impenetrable thicket;* or that a swallow was a *harbinger of spring?* They might be clichés, but when you're used to hearing about the *integral aspects of our medium-term commitment,* they don't sound like clichés. They sound colorful and gay. Hearing them might make you whistle for a week. But when did you last hear someone whistling? Possibly in Ireland; but ten years ago before the economic miracle, marketing and Sony turned the Irish people's want for Walkmans and Discmans into needs.

Ireland remains a place where there is pleasure in hearing public language spoken. It is a pocket of resistance in the empire of the English language. On the upholstery of Aer Lingus planes, slices of *Ulysses* and poems have been embroidered. William Butler Yeats's "The Lake Isle of Innisfree" spills over the back of the seat in front of you— truly a beautiful arrangement of words. If the plane went down, what would you like to enter your head in the moment before you realize death is coming at a thousand miles an hour? Hugh Grant or:

> I will arise and go now, for always night and day
> I hear lake water lapping with low sounds by the shore;
> While I stand on the roadway, or on the pavements gray,
> I hear it in the deep heart's core.

On the planes and in Irish airports announcements are made in full, flowing sentences with living words: passengers might close their eyes and think they are arriving in a hay wain. The words draw you in, at least partly because the speaker appears to take pleasure in speaking them.

If the Irish are wise and faithful to their ancestors, they will protect this language as fiercely as the French protect theirs, as fiercely as the Italians protect the genes in their tomatoes. Who knows, it might emerge as a competitive economic advantage.

Even if it doesn't turn up some improvement in the Irish *bottom line,* there will still be one airport on earth where they don't say "Due to aircraft late arrival, Flight 427 has incurred a twenty-minute delay. Qantas apologizes for any inconvenience incurred to you by this delay." Could they not say to passengers on Flight 427 something like: "Your plane was twenty minutes late arriving, so it will be a little late to leave. We are sorry for the delay, especially if it has spoiled your plans." Of course they could not. They have lost the simplest words and the simplest ability to arrange them. Soon, we can be sure, British Airways, Qantas, and all the other English-speaking airways will be asking us to *deplane,* as the Americans do.

I don't have to be cunning to write misleading sentences, or illiterate to write dead or vapid ones. I need only be inadequate or unthinking. You cannot write well if you are oblivious to the requirements and possibilities of writing. An untrained painter has more chance of creating something tolerable or interesting than a writer who does not respect the rules of language or cannot be bothered with the rudiments. The rules are not unbreakable, but they are necessary. There can be no progress—and little joy—without sometimes ignoring or breaking them. Yet they do hold it together. It's much as John Huston said of the rules, or the grammar, of filmmaking: "They must, of course, be disavowed and disobeyed from time to time, but one must be aware of their existence. . . ."

Take rhythm. Some mastery of sentence structure creates at least the possibility of rhythm in the language. So when did you last hear someone in public life who was not a rapper speak with rhythm? When did you last sense it in a letter from your bank manager? (Well, you probably don't have a bank manager; but if you do, he will not write the way the old ones used to.) Your bank manager—or whatever name his approximation goes by—will have been trained in managerialism, and you can't have both managerialism *and* rhythm in your sentences. Managerialism exterminates rhythm along with clarity and vigor.

You can be sure your bank person will not be able to write something that reads half as easily or with as much force as this four-hundred-year-old translation from various "original sacred tongues": *If a man die, shall he live again? All the days of my appointed time will I wait, till my time come.* Few bank managers ever wrote as well as this; yet there is plenty in it to imitate and, consciously or unconsciously, once upon a time they did. In fact, most people who were required to write imitated those cadences. It was possible for a bank manager to be conscious of the beats in language, of the structure of sentences, and of the potential and even the sacredness of language. Such people existed until quite recently, perhaps no more than twenty-five years ago. Coincidentally, their numbers declined not just with the rise of managerialism, but also with the fading of the King James Bible. Even so, if they knew the rudiments, they would see the same sort of rhythm in writers who might be more to their taste, like Elmore Leonard:

> It looked like Tommy had been shot in the head, only one shot hitting him of the five Chili could still hear and count, but the one was enough. Chili stood there not saying a word.

Not everyone can write like this. It's harder than it looks. But everyone who enjoys it can learn from it, and no one who knew anything about language ever said there was one kind of writing for Elmore Leonard and another for an annual report. Someone made that up, and that someone was the progenitor of this:

> To this end, the project team have undertaken a detailed testing strategy that unfortunately resulted in some unexpected results on key components of the HR module, as such we determined that it was more appropriate to defer the project by two weeks and resolve some of the open issues in a development environment rather than migrate them into a production system and try to resolve them through a support period.

Maybe if we were more conscious of the language we wouldn't let them get away with it. Grammar might help. It might even be seen as essential civic instruction: it might put language back in the picture, among the *key strategies* and *core values* and, indeed, *enhanced communications*.

And yet, while good grammar should be encouraged, cultivated, and hoped for, bad grammar is sometimes more stimulating. Bad grammar can make us laugh, for instance, whereas perfect grammar is frequently the vehicle, if not the foremost weapon, of the pedantic, the humorless, and the platitudinous. Much good writing is not as grammarians would have it. Much inspiriting speech is horrifying to their principles. When a young couple stops me in the park so they can stroke my dog, and one of them says swooningly, "Jeez, his fur is soft as," I know exactly what he means and like it much more than I would have liked some threadbare simile an older person might have added. Soft *as silk, as down, as a baby's bottom.*

You hear it all the time now—*cool as, heavy as, stupid as.* Who knows if it comes from their hating similes, or from not being able to think of them? And who cares when it's amusing? We would not want to declare "as" henceforth something more than a conjunction, but that's the point—grammar has nothing to do with it. Grammar is not where good writing starts: the word is, and the thought provoking it, or the thought it provokes.

An airhead is no less an airhead for having a command of grammar, and a liar is no less a liar. Far from it; the disingenuous, the fatuous, and the deceitful are more likely to make headway if they have perfect grammar on their side. Shakespeare has Henry VI say that by erecting a grammar school "thou hast most traitorously corrupted the youth of the realm." Many others have observed that grammar is a means of keeping those without it in their lowly place.

It might strike us as a sign of cultural decline, but we can learn to live with misused words and total confusion about apostrophes: we can suffer "disinterested" for "uninterested," "fulsome" for "generous" or "full," "refute" for "reject" or "deny," and even, with great forbearance, *"of"* for *"have"* (*He might of got ten if he had of kicked straight. But there are a lot of "might-ofs" in football, as we know, Tim.*). You can count a dozen little botches of this kind on the radio or in your newspaper every day. Even the errant apostrophes can be tolerated, or solved by simply scrapping them. It is not as if the language was ever fixed, or even logical: spelling, pronunciation, punctuation, and meanings have all changed regularly. And we can hardly complain about all the new words when Shakespeare gave us many hundreds of them, including "pedant." When we read that a football coach has *strongly annunciated his club's position* or that *Iraqi boarders are being closely watched,* should we be outraged? Only if it helps us through the day. Grammar is a concern only when it gets in the way of having, expressing, or understanding a thought or perception.

The first draft of this book began: *This is a book about the English language but not about English grammar.* In the current climate it is a wonder I did not write: *This is a book about the English language, but hopefully not about English grammar.* "Hopefully" is the most recent secular representation of God: it has replaced "God willing," and may be counted as more evidence for the theory that language profits from a deity. Some grammarians will point out that "hopefully" is an adverb, meaning *with hope,* which makes nonsense of my sentence, just as it does when a footballer says, *Hopefully it* [the ankle or groin] *will be okay by Saturday;* or a government minister says *We're sending troops, but hopefully they will not be needed.* If only the minister had said, *But we hope they will not be needed. . . .* Why did he not say *we hope?* Why doesn't anyone say *we hope?*

The worst damage, however, is done not by the grammatical flaw but by the word's overuse. For those living through a plague, it hardly matters if the pests are locusts or grasshoppers; what depresses is the number of them. "Hopefully" has become a pestilence. Panting sportsmen, pop stars, vox-popped witnesses to crime and disaster, politicians, and talk-show hosts sprinkle it into every second sentence. On some days the Australian cricket commentator Keith Stackpole may exceed this ratio, and is even heard to combine it with *in terms of*—as in: *Hopefully in terms of the batting the English might improve somewhat, Tim.*

If people need to learn or recall the principles of grammar, they need only go to Strunk and White's *The Elements of Style* or Fowler's *Modern English Usage.* Years ago, Strunk and White noted how *in terms of* had crept into the language and urged us to forgo such *padding.* Padding is no longer an adequate description. Like the cane toad that kills and substitutes itself for all other species in its path, *in terms of* has wiped out prepositions and participles, corrupted sentences, and has made much conversation hideous. It is everywhere, from the nation's highest offices to its lowest, throughout the realms of business and the civil service, on the radio, in the street—and in sport, of course.

The president of the United States is not immune: his father, he says, is the "wrong father . . . to appeal to *in terms of* strength." The Met Office says, "In terms of rain falling in a short period this was a once in a hundred year event."

Casualties are often high *in terms of* dead and wounded. And here is the Australian trade minister telling us how things are going with a Free Trade Agreement between Australia and the United States:

> They're moving things around the different baskets, but it will be the endgame in terms of putting numbers in square brackets in terms of tariff reductions, if there's significant requests on time frames in terms of phase-in.

In the wrong hands this sort of language could be used to extract confessions or incite suicide missions. It is too charitable to say that the words are merely superfluous: they are superfluous in the way that cement boots are superfluous to a man in the water. Of course, we can expect ex-footballers and ex-cricketers (and ex-accountants) to murder the language sometimes. They can easily be forgiven, and even thanked for the life and ingenuity they bring to it. Yet we are entitled to wonder why they prefer these tortuous constructions to something like, *I hope the English batting improves, Tim*—which is not only simpler and clearer but, compared with the original, sounds almost moving.

There is always something brave about a verb. When the Civil War general and United States president Ulysses S. Grant began to write his *Personal Memoirs,* he had massive debts and terminal cancer, but he wrote 250,000 words in the year he had left to him, and the work remains a literary marvel and an exemplary military history. Grant had to recount the most complex political and military events. He had to define causes and compute consequences. He did it as he had done when commanding the northern armies, when the lives of men and the fate of the Union depended

on his meaning being clear. Asked how he did it, he replied—
"with verbs."

As Lincoln used *struggled* at Gettysburg when he might
have said *engaged* in battle or *laid down* their lives, or, had he
known the modern way, *put their bodies on the line*, Grant
wrote with verbs. Of all the things we do need to know
about grammar, the verb is first.

•

Verbs are doing words. Give them up for long enough and
chances are you will stop doing anything. Just before he
died, the same General Grant wrote a note to his doctor: "A
verb is anything that signifies to be; to do; or to suffer. I sig-
nify all three." If I want to insure against the chance that I
will do something despite myself, I should say what I mean,
and write *I hope I have not written a book about English gram-*
mar. I should use a verb.

If we ever decide to take grammar seriously again, we
may as well bring back elocution, which is its distant relation. Elocution would be worth the trouble if it did nothing more than exterminate the rising inflection. Great
numbers of Americans, Australians, Canadians, and New
Zealanders these days turn all their sentences into questions
with this fiendish contrivance. No sentence or sentiment is
immune. Simple ones, like *I was really pumped?* Or *She had*
a gun? And she blew his head off with it? More complex
thoughts—*My girlfriend thinks Russell Crowe's a hunk? But I*
think he's an asshole?—may be expressed as two queries in
one. Theorizing is possible: *It's a small world? And global-*
ization sort of makes it smaller? The style suggests doubt,
timidity, fear of the categorical, awareness that the mind's
grasp of reality is tenuous, and the possibility of a fourth di-

mension must never be discounted: *Just because we can't see it doesn't mean it's not there?*

There is a theory that the tendency developed among baby boomers when they lost God and took to marijuana and sociology. Add to the mix Foucault, Derrida, and others beyond the grasp of most young minds but generally rendering belief into something much more relative, and you have a plausible explanation for the problem. *Hopefully,* a reflexive wave to personal humility and unknowable Fate, may have sprung from the same sources. *Hopefully, someone will be able to prove God's real one day?* Until they do, we might wonder if *the word* and the inflection do not betoken an attempt to impart some energy or meaning to words that profoundly lack these qualities. It doesn't work, of course. As Elmore Leonard said, we should use exclamation marks every hundred thousand words or so. He means that no device, including gratuitous queries, can raise words from the dead.

Sport is particularly fertile, notwithstanding the invention and vigor it also brings to the language. Nothing breeds clichés like sport, unless it is film and television and celebrity and news and business. Just as we imitate Tiger Woods's golf swing or someone's sidestep or cover drive, we imitate the sports journalists and presenters, and the sports journalists and presenters imitate each other. We are like those lost parrots that know they must join another flock or die. Imitating sounds is instinctive and irresistible.

In his autobiography, Czeslaw Milosz writes of a childhood Latin teacher whose classes were "a Renaissance art of the beautiful arrangement of words." At his Catholic school in Vilnius, students spent as much as an hour translating a single line of verse until they found the most precise, suggestive, beautiful meaning. In these hours, Milosz says, he learned that "what one says changes, depending upon how one says it." There is not much else to envy in Milosz's pre-war Lithuanian childhood, but I envy him that education in words.

We might envy it all the more when we watch the evening news, read the newspapers, listen to our political leaders, or read a letter from the water company. True, our schools teach that words are capable of different meanings; but they are inclined to say that the difference is made less by the arrangement of the words than by the context in which the words are written, or spoken, and, most particularly, heard. It is an axiom of contemporary discourse that *context* is everything. Whole courses are dedicated to demonstrating the interdependence of text and context—to deconstruction. This is a useful skill. But the skill of connecting words, which is no less useful and surely comes first, is taught nowhere near as widely. Indeed, students of English are more likely to study a film or a television series than anything from the literary canon: everything being a text, everything qualifies. *Hamlet* and *Who Wants to Be a Millionaire* have an equal claim on the modern student's attention: inevitably, in some schools *Hamlet*'s claim is smaller.

English teachers are expected to tell their students how to select *appropriate forms and features, and structures to explore and express ideas and values*. There is nothing in this gush to suggest that in words and their arrangement an idea is sometimes born. Yet people who write know that very often the creative context is the writing itself. Writing is the handmaiden of thought but, as Karl Kraus insisted, it is sometimes also the mother. You must know what is in your mind when you start, but once started, you cannot know in every case what you will come upon.

What happens in schools may happen for different reasons, but it's very like what happens in business and politics. It is no doubt useful to teach children the art of deconstruction. But even if we allow that structuralism, poststructuralism, and postmodernism are invaluable ways of seeing, they are useless if students of ordinary ability do not understand them and cannot see with them. And they are worse than useless if teaching them means not teaching in a way that fosters love for literature and language. Deconstruction is not another word for incomprehensible—or for managerial. But as practiced on teenagers now it is just that, and fits neatly with the communications revolution, the managerial revolution, the information revolution, the globalization revolution—with our age, in other words.

The Australians of my generation were granted a high school and university education that depression, war, and an absence of state schools had denied our parents. Our stroke of luck seems more marvelous whenever I see the modern curriculum and course guides: not only did we get an education, and a cheap one, but ours had a broader and more inspiring sweep than the one served to our children. No one had thought to call public investment in education an investment in *social capital,* as if this was the only way to justify it. Our schooling retained more than a ghost of the idea that an education for education's sake was justified and had nothing to prove in the marketplace. No one had even thought of Media Studies, Cultural Studies, Women's Studies, or Communications. We were not expected to *develop knowledge and understanding of the ways in which language forms, features and structures shape meanings in a variety of textual forms,* as one current English syllabus describes contemporary requirements. Our teachers still believed in language.

A text was still an instructional book, a context nothing more than another word for circumstances.

Naturally not everyone was satisfied by these pure purposes. Shakespeare, history, and foreign languages were all an offense against the utilitarian strain in the culture, and all were casually derided by just about everybody, including slow-witted or hormonally deranged youths wanting an excuse to leave. The dogma of *vocational education* was never far away. We had no chance of getting Latin or Greek, not in the state schools. We spent a few hours on Latin roots and a term on *Antigone,* and that pretty well did for the classics. As for grammar, women of unwavering forbearance taught it as a component of the subject called English Expression. My memory, and the unsureness of my grammar, both tell me that it did not impress itself upon us greatly. Perhaps the curriculum should have allowed more time for something so important, but I suspect the problem was less in the system than in us. That we lacked motivation had something to do with puberty and sport. But our teachers also had to contend with that general contempt for knowledge that was not *useful*.

Grammar was useful to the extent that it was useful to be understood. There was no harm in knowing how to write a good sentence, especially if you had a bit of a bent for it. But it was not an essential skill unless you intended to be a teacher yourself. This was rural Australia, and necessity governed the mind of it.

Australian pragmatism is not always a good friend of the Australian language. We might occasionally rise to heights of laconic grace and invention, but everyday language was a sort of forcing tool—like a crowbar or hammer, a practical implement with which one might improvise, el-

egantly if you had pretensions but more often brutally. Our
teachers stared bravely at our sullen, distracted faces and no
doubt pretended to themselves that one day we would be
grateful for knowing the difference between a subject and a
predicate. They might have gone as far as transitive verbs,
but if they did, I forgot them long ago. Some of us were curious or dutiful enough to learn the rudiments, but not
much more. The *arrangement of words,* like the arrangement
of flowers, was at best something to occupy the feminine element. For thinking beyond the rule of necessity, one can
never thank one's teachers enough.

If we picked up a feeling for the language it was in English literature—in the English and Australian poets (we
studied Hope and Wright but not Eliot and Yeats); in the
Austen and Dickens we labored through; but especially
Shakespeare. Shakespeare was the best thing they gave us.
Julius Caesar, Macbeth, King Lear, and a couple of the sonnets
burrowed their way in and took up residence in our inhospitable souls. We never saw the plays performed or even
heard them read, but the words came off the page and
stuck. It was the one hint we had that there were mysteri-
ous powers in language: that beautifully arranged words
could liberate, possess, bewilder, and intoxicate. They contained revelations. They could extend a person. There was
pleasure just in reciting them. Standing on the pedals of
your pushbike, grinding your way up the hill to home,
panting: "Tomorrow and tomorrow and tomorrow/Creeps
in this petty pace from day to day/And all our yester-
days . . ." "Cowards die many times before their deaths."
"Let me have men about me that are fat." "Out, vile jelly!
Where is thy luster now?"

If I could write the curriculum, I would begin with language: from the first hour of the first day at school, and every day thereafter for twelve years, children would study *the beautiful arrangement of words*. If at the end of their schooling they could not understand the language of their likely employers, I would feel that some of education's duty had been done. Innocence might have prevailed a little longer, and with it hope that the corporate muck could be discarded by a populace in love with the real language. Saved from the advanced objective of modern English to *know and understand the purposes and effects of a range of textual forms in their present social, historical, cultural, and workplace contexts,* they might remember poetry, drama, and ideas, remain aware of the word's potential, and loathe dead language all their lives.

•

In institutions where we might expect the most resistance the capitulation is most complete. Managerialism came to the universities as the German army came to Poland. Now they talk about *achieved learning outcomes, quality assurance mechanisms,* and *international benchmarking.* They throw *triple bottom line, customer satisfaction,* and *world class* around with the best of them.

The university might have no plausible claim to be among the best in the world. The terms might not describe the normal concerns of knowledge, education, and research. The words might not mean any sensible thing. No matter. Those who insist that the words *should* mean something can take the redundancy package and motor off in their old Volvos. They can sit out their lives reading Plato and drinking cheap claret while the real academics get on with teaching *customers* and *strategizing at weekend retreats, workshops, conventions, think tanks, and brainstorming sessions.*

It is hilarious. What is truth? Bah! Socrates or Plato? Kant or Nietzsche? Does it really matter? The debates at the center of Western civilization are now truly academic because they cannot be conducted in the language of managerialism or taught under managerial criteria in universities. Not only is managerial language an inadequate tool with which to explore these fundamental questions about the nature of truth, it has no respect for them. It is not a language for serious inquiry or explanation, or even for thinking.

As Rob Watts, an Australian academic, has written, the university defines itself in language more imbued with the spirit of public relations than truth-telling. When we read a university's assessment of its graduates we know what he means. According to their *Program Quality Management System* they will: *Act as professionals, meaning they will participate actively and innovatively in their professional and social communities of practice in the context of the developing knowledge economy.* Meanwhile they will also: *Reflect as citizens—reflect upon their actions as engaged citizens in the context of local diversity and multiculturalism, increasing globalization and the university's commitment to awareness of global sustainability and indigenous issues.* Furthermore, they will: *Learn from experience—make context-sensitive judgements that enable them to continuously develop and transform their practice and themselves.*

This is the kind of writing Orwell said was "tacked together like the sections of a prefabricated henhouse." He might have recognized a totalitarian quality as well: The sections do sound a bit like Soviet slogans. The words are of human origin, but they might also have been written by a not very context-sensitive robot programmed with all the clichés of modern prose and what passes for modern understanding. These are not just graduates: they are the New Citizens of the twenty-first century or astronauts fitted out for interplanetary travel or, let's be honest, figments of a failed imagination. It doesn't matter which, because they don't exist. Orwell's "prefabricated henhouse" prose is mandatory for modern management, modern marketing, and modern education. It is all humbug. Or, put another way, it is PR. It's marketing: it might not have a lot to do with the genuine prospects of students, but in a competitive world you need ambitions. You've got to want things. And who doesn't want to be *capable of continuous transformation* and *aware of indigenous issues*?

Marketing, as the marketeers will tell you, is *rooted in the exchange process*. Increasingly that's where universities are also rooted. And because of this they call their students *clients* or *customers* and feel free to sell the virtues of their institutions—real or imagined—like patent medicines. It is part of the business of marketing to muddy the distinction between altruism and cynicism: it is not normally given as part of a university's business to do this, but in taking on the language of marketing it risks taking on this part of its business.

Here are the words of an inquiry into an Australian state economy: . . . *universities face enormous pressures, with no sign of relief on the horizon.* Compare *the horizon* in this drab sentence to one plucked at random from Faulkner's *As I Lay Dying: The sun, an hour above the horizon, is poised like a bloody egg upon a crest of thunderheads*. We do not want the writers of a report on a state's economy to put *bloody eggs* on anyone's *horizons,* but, if only for the exercise, it would do them good to think of a simile of their own. Even if they decide not to use it, at least the effort might lead them to something better than a cliché—two, in fact, end on end.

No one who is paid to write should write in clichés. Everyone who can write is capable of something better. Just leaving *on the horizon* out of it would help. Or *no relief can be expected*.

And then (it's wonderful what happens once you start) our writer might be led to think twice about *enormous pressures*. Homer, as far as we can tell, managed not to say the Trojans were facing *enormous pressures*. Surrender the tired adjective; the universities are left facing pressures with nothing enormous in the way of them, and at once you see that, in general, pressures are not something you face. Pressures tend to bear down on you. They're a kind of invisible weight. Pressure crushes. That's why we say we're *under pressure—under* is better than *face* even if it leaves us for a moment with something very like a cliché. And if we say *under pressure* we might be led to say that it's like a *vise* and the *vise* is tightening and no one is going to loosen it. You might say the universities are *being squeezed*. You might not want to settle on *vise,* but so long as your imagination is engaged and not your storehouse of clichés, you are less likely to write the passage that follows:

> These pressures include substantially reduced funding, unfavorable demographic trends, and impending initiatives, which, along with reform, may present threats. Added to these pressures is the desire for the universities to be more integrated in the overall economic development strategies of the state.

You get this far and all you know is that any moment now they'll be talking about *challenging environments* and *identifying core issues* and *key issues* (not to say *key tasks*) and the need for *strategic models;* and that some progress has been made in *deriving synergies between the separate entities; but the pace of reform must be accelerated.* In this instance they *are* soon talking about such things, of course. Yet these phrases no more describe what is needed and what is happening in universities than they do what is happening in deep space: if they did describe it, nothing is needed and nothing is happening because nothing is what they describe. Therefore the writing is useless and the writers should not be paid; but the writers are likely to tell you they were told to write these things by the experts who investigated the *enormous pressures.* Surely this can't be true: they are businesspeople, experts, politicians.

It can only mean that writing and thinking are, if not the same thing, quite inseparable. If you write like porridge you will think like it, and the other way around. And if you have to read porridge all the time you may well begin to speak it, even in extremis: so when your child is killed you may tell the press, as one man did this year, that you can *only pray to God that you will have closure.* Or if your son died in battle and is buried in a mass grave, you might say, as the U.S. military imagines, that you are going to be *forever speculative on how he died* when, surely, you're always going to wonder.

Split infinitives are not the problem with public language. In its modern form there are not enough infinitives to split. They need more verbs. They need to *think* in verbs. The report on universities might have said:

The universities are under pressure. They have lost funding, and they are losing people. They struggle to keep up with the demands of reforming governments and a modern economy. True, changes have been made: they share resources and research and look for other ways to cooperate. But they must do more than this.

Put this way, nothing is lost except pomposity, jargon, and platitudes. And several hundred words that no one needed. It's hardly poetry, but it is clearer, and to that extent it lays a claim to prose. After all, as often happens with public language, we cannot see the drama in what it purports to describe: the drama that sits in all minds, even the minds of those twenty-first-century secular Methodists, the technocrats who want us to believe that life is a collection of *key issues* that can be strategically managed into *favorable outcomes.*

The subjects of the report *are* like the Trojans. To begin with, inside the walls of the universities there are people. Like the Trojans, they are people *under siege* (which is a more evocative phrase than *pressure,* even *enormous pressure*). Like the Trojans, they have something the besiegers want—not a woman in this case, but their submission certainly. Their hearts and minds? Their heads? Their souls? Something far more interesting than *creating deeper centers of excellence at each institution through greater specialization and achieving implementation success.*

Apart from clarity and shape, what we miss in these words is originality. Because there is no sign the authors have thought about the words, we are not encouraged to think about what they say. As Dr. Johnson said, "What is written without effort is in general read without pleasure." Nothing in the words suggests that the authors understand the institution they describe, or that they have a feeling for it. There is no personality or character in them. "Speak that I may see thee": but these words don't speak and we can't see.

It was not very long ago that those who ran universities and libraries defined them in their own terms, and defended them by defending learning. Now they parrot words and concepts of corporate management. But the profit from giving the name *clients* or *customers* to people who study in universities or read in libraries—or suffer *negative patient outcomes* in nursing homes—is not yet apparent.

It is possible to believe, as this refugee from academia does, that universities were rarely half what they claimed to be and badly needed dragging toward the realities of late-twentieth-century life, yet see no reason why they should give up the language of an institution of learning and take up international management-speak. Do they imagine that the new language is the necessary condition of being *world class,* and that the character of a place has nothing to do with it? That is what this writing lacks: character.

Whatever change necessity demands, universities should continue to respect the idea that truth is something worth pursuing, even when the consensus is that they cannot hope to find it. Believing only this much about the truth compels us to respect the language—and it compels universities particularly, because it is a traditional function of universities to respect language and culture, and if they don't respect it now, no one will.

At issue in the decline of public language is a principle like the one defended furiously by supporters of the seventeenth-century King James Bible and the sixteenth-century *Book of Common Prayer*. In the critics' eyes (T. S. Eliot's for instance) the twentieth-century revised versions were exasperatingly pointless and philistine assaults on a culture and history the traditional language had preserved. *Neither cast ye your pearls before swine* became *Do not feed your pearls to pigs*—and there was plenty more where that came from.

The translators of the New English Bible could not have brought more loathing on themselves if they had taken to Ely Cathedral with a Sherman tank—a good deal less in fact, because a cathedral can survive pillaging, and faith can be renewed in the rebuilding, but words once lost are gone forever.

What is more, a cathedral is the property of the church, whereas a language belongs to civilization, and (as T. S. Eliot might insist) if it is dragged down it takes civilization with it. Language is not just a preserver or bearer of tradition. Words do more than the elemental thing of linking one generation to another. The great works of public language like the *Book of Common Prayer* are poetic works. In the poetry is the mystery with which religion is concerned and on which it depends. In the poetry the inexpressible is sensed. Many churchpeople will tell you that when it adopted everyday modern prose, the church cut off an artery to its soul.

So their argument goes, and every time we hear a modern marriage celebrated we might agree. *Those whom God has joined together let no man put asunder,* the Christian service used to say, and *With all my worldly goods I thee endow.* But now they are as likely to say something about *partnerships* and *sharing everything,* and it is hard to think of a sensible reason for the change. It's not tradition we miss so much as the ring of truth. Because in the old language is the old truth, the one that the writers found in the words.

Living where he does in times like these, we can see why

Philip Roth says that all public language is a lie. But it is not so—not entirely. The *Book of Common Prayer* from which the old marriage ceremony was drawn—and by more denominations than the Church of England—was public language. Good people have lived by good public language for generations. The power of the *Book of Common Prayer* or the King James Bible lies not in its antiquity but in the conviction that the words convey. An atheist can still be moved, entertained, and enlightened by them. You can enjoy the feel of them in your mouth like a sacrament. As well as any, those works illustrate how public language should be *elevated* language: it should manifest—and honor—the traditions of the culture.

In its highest form it is exemplary language, structurally and morally. It inspires respect, encourages thought and aspiration. It unifies. *In the midst of life we are in death* are words by which for several centuries millions understood the sad paradox of existence. They are a perfect expression of our predicament, and that's why they are both majestic and comforting. The words have survived, but Thomas Cranmer (who is credited with writing them) was burned at the stake. He was devoured clutching the recantations—the falsehoods, the *political correctness*—that had been extracted from him.

Possibly, had it come to him in a vision, Cranmer would have gone willingly to the flames, bearing the Revised Version as well as the recantations. The rest of us can still ask on his behalf, what did they imagine would be gained by addressing God in the same way we address a traffic warden— as *You* instead of *Thou*? As much as we would get by turning Lincoln's classical prose, and classical endeavor to engage both the mind and the emotions, into a PowerPoint presentation, or eliding from Churchill's great speeches all the echoes of Thomas Babington Macaulay. Which is to say that nothing would be gained, but our loss would be *grievous beyond all knowing*.

Every workplace where the written language matters would be happier and more productive if no one wrote sentences like this: *These commitments are consistent with the move to more evidence-based decision-making in all natural resource management issues and will address the NCC's outstanding assessment issues regarding water reform.* And there is more to it than clarity and precision and our ability to comprehend and trust our leaders. There is the matter of the culture, of the choice between a dead language and a living one.

Not only can the public language be improved, it *ought* to be improved. Clear, precise, active language is good for democracy and for society. Active language incites activity. It helps to establish trust between the governors and the governed and the managers and the managed. Honesty and good intentions and deceit and incompetence are more easily recognized.

I make my living as a writer, and reading is a necessary and favorite pastime, so I have an interest in these matters. I stress "interest." It is not a passion, and only on one or two points does it approach obsession; just as writing is for me not obedience to an unstoppable urge or the visceral thing some writers describe. Nothing I've written would lead me to say, as Les Murray does of writing poetry, "It's done in every part of your muscles—you can feel it in your muscles." Half his luck, I say. In my muscles I feel only the lack of exercise, and occasionally fear.

And yet I know what he's getting at. There *is* a physical dimension to writing. Writing contains mysteries that only exertion can uncover. If you are possessed of rare empathy, or Keats's "negative capability," and can imagine what it's like to be a sparrow, the task will be easier sometimes. If you are master of your subject and of writing as well, so much the better. But even for geniuses there will be grueling times: for those of us less blessed, if it doesn't hurt, probably we're not trying hard enough.

We will not write as well as we can, however, if we make a meal of our deficiencies. We must not be intimidated, but find some agreeable place between awareness of our limitations and submission to them. It helps to know that experience has persuaded many average-to-good writers that while it is never possible to rise to the level of literary genius if you're not one, you can always improve. In the end everyone who writes can at least share some of a great writer's hopes. We can all, like Czeslaw Milosz, search for "our home in one sentence." Milosz discovered in his writing "an unnamed need for order, for rhythm, for form, which three words are opposed to chaos and nothingness."

In the same way, everyone who writes, including those employed in marketing, politics, and the public service, can recognize writing to which none of these words apply, and writing where chaos and nothingness rule the language that is supposed to be the enemy. Writing, in other words, that has no respect for writing. Everyone who writes can be a critic of writing. Everyone can take some responsibility— and just now, when the forces working against language seem irresistible, everyone should.

Viewed in the light of the public language, this is the starting point of my argument, the conceit on which it is built. All writers can improve, so the public language can improve. It is a question of consciousness. And necessity. If it is the right of all citizens to know, it is equally their right to be competently told.

At least with the language tacked together like a prefabricated henhouse, George Orwell was left with something recognizable and accommodating. We have a henhouse that no hen or henkeeper ever saw before or wanted to see again: an alien, inhospitable, impenetrable henhouse. It is not so much a henhouse as a cage, and we may as well be parrots in it.

•

CHAPTER 2

CORE COMMITMENTS
GOING FORWARD

•

"It is conceivable that the language of the future world will also be the purely functional means of communication that for the natural scientist it is already."
—JEAN AMERY, "HOW MUCH HOME DOES A PERSON NEED?" 1977

•

"I *implemented* the development and *enhancement* to the functionality of the existing geographic information and mapping systems by *leveraging off* opportunities within *inter-agency initiatives*."
—FROM A JOB APPLICATION

•

"•Chunk and sequence information for information for optimum digestion.
 •Become familiar with advanced language patterns and metaphors."
—LEADERVISION.COM

•

"Our ignorance exceeds our knowledge where issues of motivation and commitment of knowledge workers are concerned in the context of knowledge management systems (KMS) implementation."
—SYRACUSE UNIVERSITY OF MANAGEMENT

•

"Ten Business Values
These values reflect the ethics, goals and standards that the company and its people aspire to operate by—to achieve and sustain.

1. Placing integrity and honesty above all else.
2. Putting clients first.
3. Creating value for clients . . . etc."
—CACI HOMEPAGE

•

S IGNS OF DECAY IN THE LANGUAGE OF POLITICS AND ACA-
demia were lamented by Orwell and others in the
1940s, but today the direst symptoms are in business.
This curse has spread through the use of business models in
places that were never businesses. Universities that once
valued and defended culture have swallowed the creed
whole. Libraries, galleries and museums, banks and welfare
agencies now parrot it. The public sector spouts it as loudly
as the private does. It is the language of all levels of government, including the very local.

Your local library is now apt to speak of *focusing on the
delivery of outputs* and matching decisions to *strategic initiatives*. Almost invariably these *strategic initiatives* are *key*
strategic initiatives. In this language, schools, bank
branches, and libraries are closed down. In an education
curriculum or the *mission statement* of an international fast
food chain you will hear the same phrases. In many Australian schools eleven-year-olds are asked to write mission

statements that define their key personal values and goals. Military leaders while actually conducting wars sound like marketing gurus, and politicians sound like both of them. If one day in the finance pages you encounter *critical deliverables,* do not be surprised if it turns up the next day when you're listening to the football game. The public language has all these variants, and all of them are infected, if not dead. It is the gray death of the globalized world.

Those in the vanguard seem determined to create a new language for the new times they are bringing into being: new words to describe the new machinery, new words for the new processes, new words for leadership and management, new words to measure value and priority, new words to govern behavior; slogans to live our lives by. New technology and new commercial and industrial processes require new words, it is true. The industrial revolution was proof of this. But in this revolution the language is part of the process, part of the technology. The language is the machinery of the new age.

It is also the ideology, endlessly evolving new means of self-justification, *going forward,* as they say. Those who follow the business model—the consultant's model—follow its lead in language; and while it is partly to imitate, to impress, or to melt into the milieu, it is also because this is the language in which they are taught. Adopt the model and you adopt its terms.

In this revolution we are encouraged to take up the new, like those chimps who took up fire millions of years ago. We learn the laws of the free market as an earlier generation learned the laws of selection: that we must be competitive, that the adaptable survive and the rest are swallowed up. We are so thoroughly persuaded that everything depends on adapting to the new that we are letting go of the language for no better reason than that it is very old.

Consider these two sentences. They are not the worst specimens ever seen, but they are typical of the kind. The writer seeks applications for a job in marketing.

> Due to the nature of our industry and also the breadth of our core business offering, we have a large list of blue chip clients. Cocky Marketing has a unique positioning in the marketplace and intends to grow upon this in the coming years.

The successful applicant, the advertisement continues, will possess *an eye for detail, ability to multitask, creativity, confident ability to communicate, amicable personality, and ability to drive manual vehicle*. The language could lead us to wonder if the person advertising does not lack at least the first four skills. Yet the people who respond to the advertisement are not likely to notice any shortcomings. This kind of writing is now endemic: it is learned, practiced, expected, and demanded.

Grammar is not the problem. To work on the grammar is like treating a man's dandruff when he has gangrene. The thing is systemically ill. It will not respond to any form of massage or manipulation. You try surgery and when you've finished there's more on the floor than on the table. Look again and you realize it has been a corpse all along. It is composed entirely of dead matter, except perhaps for the bit about the *blue chip clients,* whatever they are. Leave it at *We have a large list of blue chip clients and* (if you must) *a unique position* (no *ing*) *in the Australian marketplace* and this simple sentence looks almost heroic. It might be hogwash, but it's plainer hogwash, and it doesn't turn to fog the instant it makes contact with a reader's brain.

You will see writing of this kind wherever the influence of marketing and managerialism has seeped, which is to say pretty well everywhere. It is the language of both private and public sectors, of McDonald's, your financial institution, your library, your local representative, your national intelligence organization. It comes through your door and your phone: in letters from public utilities, government departments, local councils, your children's school, banks, insurance companies, and telephone companies, all of them telling you that their main purpose is to *better address outcomes for all our customers to better achieve our goals.*

It will be put before you in PowerPoint presentations; it will blurt across your computer screen—sometimes with a friend's name and e-mail address at the top. Sometimes you will see that you have written it yourself. At any moment of the working day the screen might remind you that you are employed to *validate logic models for assigning accountabilities.* In hybrid forms it issues from the mouths of commanders of armies and leaders of nations, as if to say that in our advanced societies, government and war, like all other enterprises, come down to marketing or marketing *events.* We may be sure that in certain influential quarters there are people who believe that this is why we are so advanced.

This blurring of the corporate (or managerial) with more traditional (or primitive) human activity creates confusing environments for players. Just as a parrot might screech all day for half a century, "Where's my other sock?" as if socks mattered to a bird, a politician will now talk about promises being *core* and *noncore,* as if these business categories mattered to a promise. In the same way, teenage

46

basketballers are told to be *accountable* as if they were global corporations. Footballers and cricketers are also told to be *accountable,* and in postmatch interviews declare that because they were, they won. So far no one has been heard to say that they played *transparent* football, but recently an Australian football commentator told the listening public that the *bottom line* of entering the forward line was *validation by the leg.* And it probably is, *at the end of the day.*

It is likely that nothing attempted outside the corporate world can change what is happening to the language within it. The management revolution will continue, the corporation will continue to evolve, and the language will evolve with it. The relationship is systemic. Management language has been changing ever since the first stage of the "management revolution" in the 1930s, when managers started to be more important than proprietors, control more important than ownership. Billy Wilder's 1960 film *The Apartment* was in part a satire on the command and control structure of management and the verbal fashions that went with it. Company employee Jack Lemmon tacks *wise* onto every second word—*companywise, controlwise, lending your apartment to your superiors to have affairs in-wise.* No one works or talks like that anymore. They say *in respect of, in regard to,* and *in terms of.*

The change is foreseen in another masterpiece of those years, Vladimir Nabokov's *Lolita.* The principal of Lolita's school tells Humbert Humbert:

> . . . we are more interested in communication than composition. That is, with due respect to Shakespeare and others, we want our girls to *communicate* freely with the live world around them rather than plunge into musty

old books. . . . We think, Dr. Humbert, in organismal and organizational terms. . . . What do we mean by education? . . . we live not only in a world of thoughts but a world of things. . . . Words without experience are meaningless.

The principal wanted to leave out of Lolita's education what the modern manager and communications teacher leave out: namely, the human mind—the thing that arrives at meaning through language and will not, without coercion or deceit, reduce to a cog in a machine or an item of organization. Nabokov's principal has triumphed absolutely.

In today's *leading edge* companies, *networks* have replaced the vertical hierarchies of forty years ago; directives have given way to *communications* within and between the *networks*. This new model, we are told, makes for much faster decision-making, essential in modern global companies built around products, customers, and geography: so much faster that managers are *nodes*. *Communications* bounce off these nodes in *horizontal flows* across *silos*. Nodes are "what it is all about," the experts say: *nodes* and *networking between silos*. The essential difference between *leading edge* companies now and companies in the days of *The Apartment* is that in the old days only the top end of the hierarchy had daily need of communicating: now just about everyone in the company does. In the company, as at Lolita's school, people do not talk about language, or English or grammar or expression—they talk about *communications*.

•

Whether they talk more than they actually need to is the question. Some employees will tell you that they are run off their feet doing nothing, and that all the words exchanged in *workshops* and meetings and *dialogues* and e-mails are pointless. One former employee on the communications team of a major Australian bank estimated that seven out of every eight hours were spent pretending with her colleagues that they were busy. For this purpose the language is admirably adapted: keep talking about *strategy* and *values* and *implementation* and *going forward with your key performance indicators,* keep *workshopping* and *dialoguing* and *monitoring* and *impacting* and *having outcomes* and you'll go home as a person on your salary in a *dynamic change-driven organization* should, exhausted. Just moving language like that around the office is enough to tire anyone out.

This is a radical change. The new model, a McKinsey's heavyweight tells us, "should liberate the company from the past." Certainly it liberates the company from the language of the past, which means a lot of people are liberated from the language of their parents, much as the inhabitants of Babel were liberated by God when he confounded them. Judging an employee's performance, for example, comes down to this:

> The role of the corporate center is to worry about talent and how people do relative to each other. Workers build a set of intangibles around who they are. If they are not appreciated for their value-added they will go somewhere else.

Ask yourself: would you stay if your *value-added* was not appreciated?

The global company is the spearhead and exemplar of management change. We can presume that it will become, if it has not already, the *paradigm,* the *benchmark,* the *world's best practice,* the *KPI (key performance indicator)* of all KPIs, which means that within a year or two your football team will imitate it, as presently it imitates the fashion for *paradigms, benchmarks, KPIs, accountabilities,* and (seriously, they have been heard to say it) *best practice.* With football teams as with any organization, the argot cannot be separated from the way things are done, on the field and off it. The teams run to the principles of the *bottom line;* the players come and go according to the same principles; their worth is measured by statistical analysis that judges if their KPIs are satisfactory, if *benchmarks* have been reached. The players talk to the media in these terms. It is almost certain that they talk to each other in them. Subtle changes come over their behavior and over the game—just as they come over universities and gas companies when they succumb to management philosophy.

It's all fashion, of course, and fashion is imitation. Wherever modern management goes, however, the fashion for *networking* makes imitation compulsory. Communication is the primary purpose of a network. Everyone in the network communicates in the same language, everyone thinks in it, and no one, it seems, thinks about anything else, except, perhaps, to wonder if their *value-added* has been noticed relative to other network members'. There is at least a hint here that more than business might be going on in the *silos.* A little ambition, a little envy, a little of the kind of thing that went on in the dark ages of *The Apartment.* We can hope.

Schools of communications have appeared all over the globe, and manuals on *communication skills* proliferate to feed them. Some of these manuals make the point that people teaching communications are often the hardest people on earth to understand, that schools of communications are the worst places for jargon. The better manuals are models of clarity, and clarity is what they want their readers to achieve. They encourage short sentences, the active voice, and nouns and verbs without adjectives and adverbs fending for them: simplicity, directness. Jargon they properly despise. Structuralism, poststructuralism, postmodernism, and other fashionable academic theories are put to the torch along with similes, metaphors, and figures of speech in general. (There goes the torch.)

This may seem to fit George Orwell's austere mold, but it is also a bit silly. If a theory is incomprehensible, it is useless; and if it defies comprehension, a description of a sunset or a centaur is also useless. True, theory is more likely to be incomprehensible than description, but theory also has the potential to be more useful and stimulating. For instance, it can help us see the flaw in thinking there is little more to the writer's task than matching words to the things they describe. There is an appealing simplicity to the idea, yet it is also as fanciful as any "theory" ever was, and a doctrine to rob language of its subtle powers and splendor. To teach the doctrine robs students as well. It is one thing to feed them only chops, much worse to tell them that chops are all a lamb comprises.

It is true, one communications textbook says, that the admirable Shakespeare used figures of speech: "In Shakespeare's time, however, language of this kind was common to everyday speech, and thus natural to the period." And sure enough, we open Francis Bacon, who lived in Shakespeare's time, and at once we find him saying that a wrong done out of ill nature is "like the thorn or briar, which prick

51

and scratch"; and just a couple of lines on "cowards are like the arrow that flieth in the dark." These days, the textbook says, we don't speak or write like this. We speak plainly, or aspire to do so. Rarely as plainly as Bacon, however. Bacon, "the first that writ our language correctly," for the most part wrote plain English. Shakespeare was colorful; Bacon was plain. It seems, after all, that there was no one way to write in the seventeenth century. And in truth there never has been.

On balance, the influence of these communications manuals is likely to be good—at least for communications. The best kind of writing, they suggest, is writing we don't notice (and how pleasant it would be not to notice much of the writing one has to read). To communicate by writing—or by public speaking—is to convey information accurately and precisely. It is the effect of the information that matters, not the effect of the words. After all, this is an information society, not a word society. Should the information ever become more stimulating, it will be heaven. In the meantime, however, the utilitarian doctrine propounded in communications manuals offers little comfort or enjoyment.

Prose that is clear and precise is always better than the prolix or purple kind. But language is capable of expressing more than information: it is a medium of the imagination and the emotions. "We make all our relationships by talk, all our institutions, all our roles," as the historian and ethnographer Greg Dening says. We do not make these relationships with information alone. We use words not only to describe what we know but sometimes also to discover what we don't know. No one would recommend a manual of communications that dealt mainly in figures of speech or "flowery words." Equally, no one with a feeling for the language can recommend improving it by proscribing all adornment and adventure. No one with a care for people either, no one who believes that in the information age life might be defined by more than information.

One day perhaps someone will be interested enough to trace the point at which this journey into fog began. Was it the Chicago School of Economics? Was it the management revolution? Microsoft? (No one *enhances* like the IT business.) Whenever it was, the overlap between political and business language became a merger in the early 1980s when economics—free market or supply-side economics—became so brutally the main game of politics. In the years since then, business language has been steadily degenerating, mauled by the new religions of technology and management. But its range now spreads well beyond politics and the corporations, and into all the corners of our lives.

The same depleted and impenetrable sludge is taught in schools of marketing and business. And, significantly, it is taught in groups, in conscious or unconscious anticipation of the *teams* that corporate management favors. Few teaching strategies could do more to discourage fluency or independent thought. Combine this with the requirement that every "thought" comes with a parenthetical reference to some authority, when every authority is written to the same formula and in the same style, and you guarantee in student essays an exhausting, intellectually vacuous admixture of jargon, cliché, and undigested plagiarisms that is perfectly suited to life in modern organizations. Put another way, you have corporate doctrine, doctrinally taught.

If, in your professional life, you want to understand your fellow human beings and be understood by them, begin with a mission statement. And remember, everything worth putting on paper, slide, or disk has a dot in front of it. It should look something like this:

What We Stand For: *Our Core Beliefs and Values*
- *Objectivity is the substance of intelligence, a deep commitment to the customer in its forms and timing.*

Don't worry if you're not entirely sure what this means. Once you have mastered the style, you are halfway to the philosophy, which is why the easiest way to write a mission statement is to borrow someone else's. Any sort of outfit will do: a supermarket chain, a public service department, or an intelligence organization. The one quoted above is the CIA's. The dot point following the previous one is:

- *Intelligence that adds substantial value to the management of crises, the conduct of war, and the development of policy*

If you continue to use the CIA model—but McDonald's would do just as well—mention, as they do, *accountability, teamwork, commitment, continuous improvement,* and *adapting to evolving customer needs.* If Margaret Thatcher was right and there is no such thing as society, it must be that we live in an economy, and in an economy, what are we if not customers? We are all customers now, even in many of our universities, hospitals, and libraries, where we used to be readers. The Inland Revenue calls us customers. Friends, Romans, customers . . . Of the customer, by the customer, for the customer shall not perish from the earth.

When I told the telecommunications company that I was transferring my account to its rival, a reply came addressed *Dear Valued Customer.* They asked me to *accept our sincerest apologies for any inconvenience or frustration the billing issue, raised may have caused. We constantly strive to give our customer's [sic] our best service experience and it is of some concern to us to hear that your expectations were not met by us in this instance.*

It is not the misplaced comma and apostrophe that kill these sentences. It's the *billing issue,* the *service experience,* and the glue in the next sentence: *constantly strive, some concern to us, in this instance.* The aim is to sound polite and helpful, but the result is unctuous, unhelpful, and depressing. You cannot get through such prose. And subliminally at least, that is the bigger message: *you cannot succeed in this.* Submit. Roll over. The language of corporations is like a vampire without fangs; it has no venom or bite but you don't want it hanging off your neck just the same.

Modern public language handcuffs words to action, ideas to matter, the pure thought to the dirty deed. It collapses the categories for the sake of convenience. What you think and what you are become one, the customer (or the client), and it is for your custom—your patronage—that you are *valued.* In your other life, as an employee of a *customer-focused organization,* you are a member of a *team,* a team where everyone has learned to think the same thoughts, or at least within the same *parameters.* If these parameters are defined by what is called *Knowledge Management* (KM), very likely they encompass a *knowledge entity: Knowledge entities are incomplete if they do not cultivate a dialog between the members of the community of practice to advance the defining and refining of a socially constructed process. Knowledge Management* is one more mutant form of the managerialism marching over a whole tradition of Western philosophy, crushing all subtleties and distinctions.

Verbs are ground out of existence, nouns driven into

service as a substitute for them; all but a few adjectives (*robust, vibrant, enhanced*) are abandoned, along with metaphors because they are untidy distractions from the main objective, which is a serviceable instrument of communication. "First the adjectives wither, then the verbs," Elias Canetti said.

All elegance and gravity have gone from public language, all its light-footed potential to intrigue, delight, and stimulate our hearts and minds. We use language to deal with moral and political dilemmas, but not this language. This language is not capable of serious deliberation. It could no more carry a complex argument than it could describe the sound of a nightingale. Listen to it in the political and corporate landscape, and you hear noises that our recent ancestors might have taken for Gaelic or Swahili, and that we ourselves often do not understand. Even some of those who speak and write it will tell you that they don't know quite what it means. Then again, this is less a language to be spoken or written than a language to be *implemented*.

•

The public realm has been in decline since governments retreated from the direct control of the economy and private companies moved in to take their place. The operation extends well beyond privatized public utilities in gas, water, electricity, and transportation. Economic revolution has transformed our institutions—colleges and universities, hospitals and medical practices, the public service itself—and transformed our relationships with them in doing so.

As private enterprise absorbs the public realm, it finds itself obliged to pick up social functions and responsibilities that traditionally belonged to governments. It picks them up in different ways, and it uses a different term for them: what the state called "social services" it calls *investing in social capital* or *corporate social responsibility* (CSR).

The terms betray a different conception of the role, a shift from service to service aligned with profit, and therefore with marketing, branding, image. Private enterprise tells its *stakeholders* that it is not only their duty to society to show a little care for the downtrodden and the environment, it is also good for business. What remains of the public system follows the corporate lead—indeed, becomes more "corporate" than the corporates. Thus people who spend the nights in subways, people addicted to heroin or alcohol, people with Alzheimer's disease, schizophrenics, and prostitutes become *customers* and *clients* of *customer-focused* health departments.

The old bureaucratic—*yours of the 4th inst.*—forms were pompous, obscure, and prolix. Sir Ernest Gowers's *Plain Words,* Fowler's *Modern English Usage,* and centuries of satire were necessary to decode and knock the stuffing out of them. But at least there was stuffing to be knocked out. Generally there was a meaning to be divined, something worth saving. And there was room within this official language for elegant exceptions, a drollery, a little tartness, sudden and unexpected flair. I know people who while working in the old bureaucracies read much of the literary canon, including Joyce and Kafka, in their spare time. The thought is horrible to any modern organization, yet no one can prove that their study was not public time and money well spent.

James and J. S. Mill wrote books that changed the course of history while working for the East India Company, a multinational. Not today they wouldn't. Today they would be attending countless meetings, seminars, and conferences to update their knowledge of work-related subjects, all of them conducted in the mind-maiming language of managerialism. And, to draw a longer bow, the more of these *fora* (*fora,* archaic plural of forum, now common in up-to-date bureaucracies and NGOs where they attend a lot of forums. *In my role as chairperson last year I attended several international fora*) people spend time in, the less likely it is that they will ever know the comfort of seeing their lives reflected in Joseph K. or Leopold Bloom or Mr. Casaubon. And the benefits of such self-knowledge and of exposure to good writing will, it follows, never find a way into their language.

That is the dire point. Bad as the old language could be, there were always cracks in it, and comprehensible, even creative, language sometimes squeezed through. Even the worst of it was always at least a variant or mutation of the language we all understood. But great lumps of the new language are unrelated to anything ever spoken. It's a kind of self-sealing grout that keeps its speakers—and meaning—unconnected and unexposed to ordinary thought and feeling: *As part of the electronic delivery strategy the vision to enable customers to transact low face value commoditized financial market instruments electronically and seamlessly.* This might mean that customers will be able to transfer money by electronic means for a reasonable price. But who can say? It might be a secret message that only their most valued (i.e., blue chip) customers understand.

The meaning aside, the sentence just quoted contains a common maneuver in corporate language, so common that if reason didn't tell us otherwise, we might conclude that it bears some connection to the way organizations actually think and act. The maneuver is with the word *strategy*. *The electronic delivery strategy makes it possible to deliver things electronically.* This is very much as we would expect: imagine our surprise if the strategy brought about seamless delivery by rowboat. We might put it down to careless repetition if the same *strategy* did not turn up in so many annual reports, mission statements, even applications for academic research.

All modern organizations (and many modern organized people no doubt) must regularly (if not continuously, in the interests of *continuous improvement*) measure their performance. This is done with KPIs. KPIs are to modern managers what the stars were to early navigation. They set their course by *strategic goals* and mark them off against results. Who knows, the method may do wonders for the *bottom line* and human happiness, but you would not think so from what shows on the page. On the page it has a crude pedagogical quality, as if designed for remedial high school students. Under a general heading of, say, LEADERSHIP, we see columns and dot points. One column is headed STRATEGIES and the other RESULTS. Under *Leadership* we get windy summaries of ambitions. The following is typical: *The Museum will be recognized locally, nationally, or internationally as an industry* [sic] *leader through the exemplary way it conducts its activities, serves the community, is accountable to government, and responds to sponsors' needs.* Under *Strategies* we read: *Through a collaborative and inclusive process, develop strategic support for regional museums throughout the state.* And in the next column under *Results*: *The committee facilitated discussions about strategies for effective collaboration and support for regional touring exhibitions.*

In such mission statements there are typically dozens of

strategies, and for each of them *results* must be found. It is no surprise that sometimes the two seem to be all but interchangeable, and there is little to persuade us that in every case the *results* are written in the light of the *strategy* and not the other way around. The *result* is something that, for all the talk of *key outputs* (read exhibitions and research) and being *a preferred provider of enjoyable and educational experiences* (visits and tours), looks less like an analysis than humbug, or a charmless parody of Soviet bureaucracy.

What you don't look like is a museum, a research institution, an institution of character. They say they want to be a *world player* (one state library says *world* three times in its mission statement, though it's not sure what to call the people, formerly known as "readers," who use the library), but they must also say they are *community- and customer-focused.* They sound, therefore, like every other organization. Whatever your business—brain research, boiled sweets, rabbit trapping, underwear manufacturing—you must be equal to the *world's best practice,* and *responsive to customer needs, strategic* (of course), and *accountable,* and so on. So you must also be prolix and utterly predictable. You are trapped in the language like a parrot in a cage.

I can think of no better demonstration of the syndrome than when, a few years ago, a politician stood on a stage in front of a troupe of modern dancers who had just completed a performance. The speech began with an appreciation of the dancers' art but soon veered toward something like he might have delivered in a car plant at the launch of a new model or to a press conference on budget night. It was a speech of the kind politicians have been giving for a decade—ever since they learned that their trade balances were fatally awry, or would be if they did not liberalize their economies at once.

Most of the good old lines were there: I seem to remember *international best practice* even found a way into it.

I also remember the dance troupe whose presence on-stage was taken to justify the politician's theme. Because they had recently been induced to leave their hometown and move to another city, they were proof of *dynamic market forces*. That a good part of their act satirized these forces was immaterial. They were good; they had been well reviewed in Europe, hence the talk about *competitiveness*. The usual mantras had been rolled out, and the chance of spontaneity reined in, and with it the politician's ability to see that the dancers' *international competitiveness* had left them in a muck sweat, detumescing and blowing like horses after a race, three-quarters naked, pulsing. It was, as they so often say in the arts, and many other places nowadays, *in terms of* an evening in the theater, quite bizarre.

In terms of is to the language what a codling moth is to an apple tree, and just as exasperating. For instance: *Both oil and high-tech sectors are characterized by "leader" and "laggard" companies in terms of environmental performance.* And all *sectors* are characterized by dead words. What need, except the need of habit or the need to sound like everyone else in the consultancy sector, is satisfied by *in terms of* in this sentence? For that matter, what good does *characterized* do? Or *environmental performance*? Couldn't they just say: *in both sectors there are companies that lead on the environment and companies that lag behind*?

Here we go again: *The U.S. was an early leader in the area of information disclosure and, in terms of government information, remains far more transparent than many European countries.* We are so used to the expression, we may not notice it at first. But look again and you see it has a grub in it. Remove the grub and you have: *The U.S. was an early leader in the area of information disclosure, and government information remains far more transparent than many European countries.* This is not precisely what you want, but once you've made the first move you can see the others, at least as far as saying *and U.S. governments are still far more transparent than many European countries.* Who knows, you may decide that *transparent* is vague and *area* is a waste of space. So you might rewrite the sentence as: *The U.S. was an early leader in information disclosure, and U.S. governments continue to disclose much more than many European countries.* You might prefer *disclosing information* to *information disclosure.* You might decide the bit about being an *early leader* is not worth the trouble. You might want to adjust the nuances, but now at least there are nuances to adjust.

Corporate leaders sometimes have good reason to obscure their meaning by twisting their language into knots, but more often they simply twist it out of habit. They have forgotten the other way of speaking, the one in which you try to say what you mean. Instead, they welcome their audience and proceed immediately to put them in a coma by announcing their intention to spend the next half hour *outlining the company's key strategies and initiatives going forward,* and their *commitment* to fill *capability gaps* and *enhance sustainable growth for the benefit of all stakeholders.*

Habit, however, is not the only thing that motivates them. They suffer from the same pomposity that afflicts most people when they write formally or make formal speeches. This may be letting many of them off too lightly: some people are pompous by nature, and if no one has ever firmly told them how unattractive it is—to read, hear, and watch—they go on being pompous all their lives. Pomposity is the verbal equivalent of wearing epaulettes and braid, or a hat with bones and feathers in it, or, because pomposity is sometimes defensive, a flak jacket.

Even when we use it as a shield against our own uncertainty, pompous language is a weapon, an expression of power. Part of it is a mistaken effort to elevate the tone. Beneath pomposity rests the assumption that she who elevates the tone will herself be elevated—with luck, beyond scrutiny. The risk, which the truly pompous never see, is that an opposite effect is achieved or the tone moves sideways into unself-conscious parody. Not that everyone will laugh when they encounter this, an example from the public sector:

> Unfortunately, due to the recent unprecedented demand for the publication *Australian Meteorological Radio Facsimile Broadcasts,* and therefore a diminution of stocks, there is now an exigency to restrict dissemination of this publication to professional end-users and institutions only.

Speakers and writers may also think it useful to keep their audience so deep in darkness, they will not be able to see the flaws, or conclude that they must be stupid not to understand. Academics, teachers, and priests are likely to recognize the same conceit in their professions. To the extent that all public performance is an effort to narrow the focus of an audience to a single point of light—from whence comes the voice of truth—public performers can be tempted to make words arcane, magical, and (why not?) incomprehensible. *Maximizing synergies* and *pushing the envelope* might satisfy some Druidic urge.

Keen to demonstrate that they are competitive and internationally benchmarked, corporations and government departments write to advise their customers that they have thought of ways to serve us better. A letter came last year announcing *some enhancements to our billing systems to serve you better*. It continued: *These recent enhancements to our billing systems may mean you receive your next bill later than usual, and you may also notice some minor format changes. All normal payment terms and conditions still apply*. Nothing else in the letter explained what the *enhancements* were, but that is the way with *enhancements*—often they don't amount to anything at all. It's just that the word *enhancement* has become irresistible, like ice cream or chicken pox. *Enhance* is the McDonald's of corporate English. The letter went on:

> We are paving the way for better, more enhanced ways of doing business, and these enhanced systems are designed to deliver on that commitment. These improvements will allow for more flexible and efficient billing options as we move forward.

Here are worn clichés and clichés freshly coined. We begin by *paving the way* and then we get *enhanced* (and more *enhanced*—four *enhance*s in fifty words) and *commitment* on which we *deliver,* and *flexible* and *efficient* and *options,* and it is all done, of course, as we *move forward*. Government documents and company annual reports of more than two pages will almost always contain these last two words. The same is true of party statements, mission statements, consultancy reports, and annual reports.

Commitment is a politician's word of the worst kind, though organizations—especially *customer-focused* organizations—now use it at least as frequently, and for the same reason. To say we are *committed* to something does not mean we believe it (if we did, why not say so?) or that we will do it (if we will, why not do so?). *Commitment* is a standard weasel word, a weed that spread with the fashion for mission statements, new management theories, and sports psychology. *Commitment* is everywhere, and has been for twenty years. One might think that life is impossible without it, that speech is impossible without it. One might also think that until twenty years ago no one had ever been committed. Yet Churchill did not talk about *commitment*, and Lincoln got through Gettysburg without it. At the heart of *commitment*, there is deceit, including self-deceit. But, as with all weeds, *commitment*'s main offense is to the landscape. It is the ugliness of it and the ubiquity. It might not fool us, but it does depress us.

Enhance can mean anything, which is why it's so popular with people who have lost the ability to say what they mean. Once, we might have said *improve* or *augment* or *illuminate*, or *accelerate*, or *lengthen*, *broaden*, or *make hairier*—any one of hundreds of verbs. Now we say *enhance*. We *enhance* our competitiveness, our hair color, our national security, our breasts, our chances, and our billing systems. We *enhance* our defense forces and our education. We *enhance* our *commitment*, and we are *committed to enhancement*. We *enhance* our children's genes, or very soon some among us will, and it's a fair bet that many who choose the path of *genetic enhancement* will have *enhanced* much else in their lives beforehand. Their computers, their kitchens, their education, their lifestyles—they may even own one of those coffeemakers that boasts a *froth enhancer*. Chances are they will see life as a succession of *enhancements;* and viewed from their particular balconies those *enhancements* will be looking very much like evidence of *continuous improvement*. It's uncanny how they coincide . . . like revealed truth, like a kind of miracle. So why wouldn't you *enhance* your kid? This language really works!

The children, of course, will overhear their parents and demand *enhancements* to their lives, *implementation* of their *plans,* and *closure* on all *issues*. If not their parents, they'll pick it up from television, where our leaders are prone to saying things like this:

> Negotiation and persuasion are just as important in maintaining agreement and focus for the significant re-forms which we have reached agreement about. The government has worked hard to cement in place the negotiated settlements it has achieved. Agreement is the easy part! Implementation takes time.

An unmistakable symptom of the modern sludge is the *buzzword*. The thing about a buzzword is that, as a word, it doesn't buzz. It might *create* a buzz, but only under certain conditions. It might buzz in the reaches of the human mind and human culture that explain the preeminence of commerce, technology, and politics in the world's affairs—but it doesn't buzz in a sentence.

Consider the buzzword *flexibility*. In another letter to me, a *valued customer,* a telecommunications company offered me a plan to provide the *flexibility to choose what best suits your needs*. When you think about it—which is not something this kind of language encourages—you see that, even if I needed *flexibility,* the sentence does not. It weighs the sentence down, and what's more, distracts the reader from the very thing it wants him to recognize—that he can choose. Instead of offering him something he can do, it offers him something he can have, *flexibility*. Why not write: *Our plan allows you to choose?* Or: *With our plan you can choose?* The noun inserts itself because somewhere in the writer's mind there is a jargon-seeking impulse that insists on inserting a *key* word, the buzzword. *Flexibility* will be there even if it kills the sentence stone dead. *Flexibility* has been, if you like, *prioritized*. It has been deemed more important than the sentence itself.

It all began when strenuously networked, compulsively imitative companies got the idea that it was necessary to be *flexible*. Modernity demands *flexibility*. It goes with supply-side economics. It also goes with globalization, with being *internationally competitive*. *Flexibility* has come to mean many things: production should be *flexible*—goods should be produced and delivered "just in time," not en masse with rigid production lines and costly warehousing. Management should be *flexible*—it should *think outside the box*. And staff should be *flexible*—they should be *multiskilled* and prepared to work hours that are *flexible*.

Governments also took up the *flexible* thing. They ran their departments, and the departments ran their agencies, as modern businesses—and modern businesses demanded *flexibility*. Deregulation and a floating currency removed certain rigidities, and the economy became more *flexible*. Soon it became obvious that the labor market would also have to become more *flexible,* so the trade unions were branded obsolescent unless they were *flexible,* and *flexible enterprise agreements* replaced *inflexible* awards. To meet the demands of the more *flexible* economy, universities and colleges became more *flexible* and rigidly opposed to anything that wasn't. The technological revolution became an information revolution, and both *enhanced* the *flexibility* of *consumer choice*. *Flexibility* is not only a precondition of success in the postmodern age, it now is also purported to describe it. The whole world, at least the affluent parts of it, which is to say the *flexible* parts, is *flexible*.

Some may think *enhanced consumer choice* has not *enhanced* existence much or cast much light upon its meaning, and some will say that, like other fads and religions, *choice* has confined life more than it has widened it. Others will tell you that they have never spent more time and money on telephony since it became a commercial contest. And even those who believe the whole telecommunication enterprise has been one of history's great *enhancers* have to concede that, whatever it has done for *flexibility,* it's done nothing for the language.

It seems that *consumer choice* expands in inverse proportion to our vocabulary. We use fewer words and words of less variety. We arrange them with less imagination and dexterity. We tangle and abuse them. We take the richest soil the culture has and turn it into a few clods. Ever since Alexander Pope and Samuel Johnson took it upon themselves to eliminate the vulgar from the English tongue, the language has been lopped at by snobs, pedants, and prudes, but nothing done to it by the Augustans or the Victorians comes close to the violence of the managerial age. It is not the worst thing that can happen to people, but it cannot be described as progress.

The buzzword is the corporate equivalent of the political "grab," the "message" inserted by politicians in a speech or at a doorstop interview regardless of the subject, the con-

text, or the questions they are asked. Savvy political advisers arm their bloke with the word or phrase, and he utters
it come what may. Opening a new nursing home, he finds
some labored pretext in the speech to say that the political
Opposition are committed to decimating [sic] *the family.* At the
doorstop the journalists will say the war seems to be going
badly, and he will say that this is mere conjecture, but there
is no doubting the Opposition's determination *to decimate
the family.* Then they'll ask if interest rates are going to rise,
and he will say that that is a hypothetical question and he
will not answer it, but there is nothing hypothetical about
the Opposition's determination *to decimate the family.* They
will ask about his recent meeting with Her Majesty and he
will say, it went very well indeed, but while he is carrying
on these affairs of state, Opposition MPs can think of nothing better than *the decimation of the family.* A news conference
is always partly a contest to determine the day's story, and
it's a contest politicians need to win, just as business needs
to win the contest for our custom with advertising slogans.
But, whoever wins, only rarely are we much enlightened by
what we see and hear.

•

Writing and painting are forms of expression that depend
on observation, imagination, and skill, so what is said about
one can sometimes also be said about the other. Not always,
however, and because there is no one way to write or to
paint, there are no rules applying to both. As most of us can
enjoy equally, say, a Velázquez and a Picasso—or a water-
color and an oil—so we might like both plain prose and
prose full of imagery:

In Theodora's world a wet finger could have pressed the cardboard church, and pressed, until the smoking sky showed through. Sometimes an iron tram careered quite dangerously along the spine of a hill. People mopping their heads wondered uneasily into what they sank in Theodora Goodman's eyes. People casually looking were sucked in by some disturbance that was dark and strange.

As a model for public language, we might prefer Orwell to Patrick White, but not if his style is taken as encouragement for government and corporate writers to stick to the familiar and stay *on message*. Plain writing need not be lifeless writing. It is useful to pare away extraneous words and flourishes for the sake of clarity, but there must be something at the end of it, at least something with a point.

There is a lesson for writers in what Delacroix said about his own favorite artist, Titian: he was

the least mannered and therefore the most varied of painters . . . he constantly defers to genuine emotion. He has to render that emotion. Embellishment and a vain show of facility do not interest him. On the contrary, he disdains everything that does not lead him to a livelier expression of his thought.

It is unlikely that a better general rule for writing was ever conceived.

Signs that the rule is untaught include the absence of civility and human sympathy in public language, or, worse, evidence that we have lost the forms of their expression. Not very long ago unsuccessful applicants for jobs received letters that concluded with the words "good luck" and "hoped" (not *hopefully*) they would meet success, and "thank you for applying." I saw these sorts of words a few years ago in a letter from a Dublin office, and they let loose in me remarkable feelings of lightness and goodwill. It should not be difficult to reinstate such simple civilities, but half a generation of deadly decline would first have to be reversed.

There might even be a clue in the changing style of music and other popular entertainments and rituals. When people write: *It is a self-regulatory agreement between the packaging chain and spheres of government, based on the principles of shared responsibility through product stewardship, and applied through the packaging chain, from raw materials to retailers, and the ultimate disposal of waste packaging,* it could be that they echo the structure of minds fashioned by din, chaos, television, and method acting. The difference between this and a coherent sentence is perhaps the difference between Humphrey Bogart and Al Pacino, Cary Grant and Hugh Grant. It's the language of twitching narcissism derived more from imitation than from art.

What we can be sure of is that once this kind of language gets inside a company, it spreads like duckweed down every channel of communication. Both private- and public-sector employees will tell you they write like this because the boss does, or because everyone else does. And because corporate and government speeches and policies are often composed by teams, or by chains stretching from a department to an office to a leader; and because nowhere on the chain, in the team or in the *horizontal flow,* is there someone with the duty to think deeply or imaginatively about the subject, and write thoughtfully and imaginatively about it, the speeches and policies are indeed nailed together in prefabricated bits like one of Orwell's henhouses, and come out as witless and unfathomable dreck. And writers down the chain will tell you that when they write in plainer or richer English, higher authorities rewrite it in the house (read *global*) style.

Of course, it can't be entirely explained as mass submission to the power of a consuming fashion, much less to psychological or anthropological forces. It is an epidemic, but one in which, surely, some choice remains. Businesses can be forgiven their neologisms, but not their *technocratic* sludge. If they can find the means to *downsize, prioritize,* and *implement quality function deployment,* they can find better words to describe what they are doing.

Their failure becomes most acute when they try to bend the language into an instrument of persuasion. The fact is, of course, it can't be bent. It is incapable of carrying mood or emotion. It can neither admonish nor praise.

When, for example, those who speak the new language wish to demonstrate their concern for the less fortunate or the less profitable, or for the community at large, they speak of addressing *the triple bottom line through corporate social responsibility,* known as *CSR.* There is nothing wrong with this idea: rich private individuals and enlightened companies have been in the business of benefactions for a very long time. Some have done it in a spirit of charity, and some have mixed charitable feelings with self-interest and as much good has come of it. Great and lasting good works have been done in this way, from mighty endowments to the arts and science of incalculable value to humankind to the socks provided by the local haberdasher for a provincial football team. Some businesses offered their employees shares in the company and a voice in the management a century ago. Some were offering pensions, child care, and training on the job. Some took care of the environment. But today the corporations, having found it is good business to be good citizens, struggle to find words to describe their good intentions. Principally this is because their language has been stripped of meaning. They don't have words like *generous, charitable, kind,* and *share;* phrases like *give and take* or *enlightened self-interest;* or even words that governments and their bureaucracies, whose roles they are usurping, once used freely—*welfare, wealth transfer, social service, social benefit, social policy, social contract.* They would no more use words like these than they would use a word like *greed.* They search for human signs in the business lexicon and come up with terms that are all at once unctuous and pompous, impenetrable and threatening. Meeting this kind of vaporing is like meeting some smiling brute from a Coen Brothers film, a psycho who seems to listen but never understands, who sits on the end of your bed and says he is *committed* to you and your family and your community and your country and to the whole world, but you wonder if he might soon go out and kill someone—or you, should you fall asleep.

> We are committed to social responsibility. We are committed to doing the right thing. We want to make a positive difference in the world. This commitment began with our founder Ray Kroc. It continues today with our Board of Directors and executive leadership, is shared by our staff and franchisees, and reaches across our front counters to our customers and their communities.

This is McDonald's. It is McDonald's Corporate People Promise. McDonald's Corporate People Promise comes with promises to animals as well. The company has established *the industry's first independent board of academic and animal protection experts. The Council has led to additional leadership initiatives for the well-being of cattle, poultry, and hogs.* But we need not pick on McDonald's. Just about every company that takes on *Corporate Social Responsibility* expresses it in much the same way—in terms of *commitments* (and *enhancements*), as in:

> We are committed to providing information to all our stakeholders in a clear and open way.

> We are committed to establishing greater transparency and access to information.

> We are committed to providing you with a quality service and will make every effort to resolve the matter you have raised.

> Commitment to these principles enhances the Department's ability to attract and retain staff, maximize staff potential, and enhance the employment climate.

> We are always working to ensure you are supplied with clean, fresh water. To continue doing this, we occasionally need to shut off your water supply.

You might want to believe them. You might even persuade yourself that you do. But there's something about the way they talk that doesn't ring true. It doesn't ring false, for that matter. In fact, it doesn't ring at all. It's the verbal equivalent of a blank stare. The word *commitment* has something to do with it: why don't they say *We will do the right thing; we will provide information; we will establish . . . ? I am committed to the future of Africa:* why don't I just look in the general direction of Nairobi and wave? It would mean as much.

But it also has something to do with taking us for mugs. It is one thing to tell people that the bun in the bag is a hamburger, but to say that the company's mission was all but *benchmarked* by the Franciscans is something else entirely. What happened to "the business of America is business?" Do they think we'll cook at home if they project themselves as anything less than selfless to a fault? It seems more likely that language is the root of it.

Here is another example of the formula:

At CACI we take pride in our commitment to:
- Quality service and best value for our clients
- Individual opportunity and respect for each other
- Integrity and excellence in our work
- Distinction and the competitive edge in our work

CACI was one of the private contractors at Abu Ghraib prison near Baghdad. In 2004, U.S. law firms filed suits on behalf of some of CACI's *clients* at the prison alleging torture and other abuses.

•

Corporate language simply doesn't have the equipment to dissemble subtly. We know how much they mean it when a letter of offer comes with the same labored attempts at niceness as a letter of demand. It is all done to *serve you better* or *enhance our services to better serve you.* A bank can't tell you that it is cutting a fee without setting this small gesture in the context of its *corporate social responsibility,* its *holistic approach* to munificence. And it can't tell you that in the future it will bounce all checks that overdraw your account by more than five pence, and hit you with a fee for doing so, without a pro forma letter that also tells you we are *changing the way we honor payments which will overdraw accounts,* and they are telling you so *we can better manage the way you do your banking with us.*

There is no space in this sanctimonious clag for the light of the imagination. There is no room for a feeling properly felt. There is no room for an "other"—which with writing is usually the reader. You cannot tell if the author of these words is genuine or not, because they have no author. They are ritual words. It is as if, like someone with schizophrenia or depression, they are not quite of the real world. They have forgotten the language the rest of us speak.

If Francis Fukuyama needs more evidence to support his theory that we are at the end of history, he might find it in the decline of public language. It will be "a very sad time," Fukuyama wrote more than a decade ago.

> The struggle for recognition, the willingness to risk one's life for a purely abstract cause, the irreducible ideological struggle that called for daring, courage, imagination, and idealism, will be replaced by economic calculation, the endless solving of technical problems, environmental concerns, and the satisfaction of sophisticated human demands. . . .

Perhaps not everyone will remember the Cold War so fondly, but it is easy to see a connection between his description of human concerns in the post–Cold War world and the language we now endure. The professional life may not yet be the *archetypal* life, but the line between the workplace and the rest of existence is no longer clearly drawn: words, ethics, and ideals are all increasingly interchangeable and, thanks to radio, television, and the Internet, pervasive.

It may be that business, especially in its global manifestation, is unself-consciously shaping a language of near-perfect objectivity, a language stripped of ambiguity and variety and possibility, including the various interpretations that words are open to. You may be as clear as a cat with a fur ball, but better to speak in buzzwords and clichés because there can be no argument with words that have no meaning at their core. Eccentric and atypical behavior among politicians—including loss of moral judgment—can often be explained by their inability to distinguish between the different codes that govern the world of business and the world of democratic government. Any politician who has to survive a difficult interview can easily be caught up in the confusion inherent in *building an online platform for integrated customer-centric service delivery;* or *adopting innovative methods for effectively chartering* [sic] *future paths for portal development and ultimately making customer interaction with government operations more effective.* You can hear them saying it, adding only that these things are not done *overnight,* but within *a reasonable time frame.*

The media is always the forcing ground. Listen to the coaches interviewed at the end of football matches and you will hear words straight from the corporate world, which is where their teams now belong: "We *zoned off*"; "We stuck to the *game plan*"; "We need more *flexibility*"; "We were com-

mitted to the ball." Before 1990, no player in the history of ball games had ever been *committed* to the ball. Now every player must be.

What we are losing is language expressing character or imagination, which interests one human being in another, and from which the game's spirit springs. It is fading at the point we would expect to see it most plainly, the panting postmatch interview. Sometimes in these brief cameos we seem to be seeing a human subject dispensing with itself— or all except the teeth and muscles. And so it is sometimes with politicians, except in their case with the suits. Is the *professionalization* of the language the apotheosis of the postmodern?

•

The sublime is within the reach of public language—listen to Martin Luther King's speech on the steps of the Lincoln Memorial in 1963, then say it is not—but it is getting further from our grasp. This is partly because politics is played on a narrower field, one where inspiration and independent thought are not encouraged. The field is defined by ideological *think tanks,* and players are professionals who work to a *game plan* or *strategy,* including the strategy of using the word *strategy* wherever and whenever they can. Another strategy might be to describe their political enemies as "elites," or never to mention them without saying "liberal." It is, of course, an identical strategy to the one that leads corporations to say *flexibility* or *customer-focused* without respite.

Words, being open to all kinds of interpretation including some that are not *on message,* are chosen only after strenuous *risk assessment*. If, like much else in contemporary politics, this sounds more like the corporate world than politics, get used to it. Political thought and speech has been entangling itself with the corporate stuff for years, and unless a way is found to separate them, in a generation or two few people will know that anything better once existed. We do not wait for Pericles, but we hope for something better from a politician than a poor imitation of a business consultant. When we read what follows, we know we have an *issue* here, a *capability gap in terms of words.*

> I have flagged with the government my involvement to assist in resolving the issues that are impeding reconciliation. I would like to progress discussion with indigenous people to set in process the parameters of reconciliation.

Consciously or not, the politician (or his adviser) was only attempting to speak the language of the locals. He was *value-adding* (or *adding alpha,* as very refined managers say). *Value-adding* is a mantra of modern economics: it describes the increase in value that a particular manufacturing process or design or labeling or some other *enhancement* brings to a product before its sale. Those who talk a lot about *value-adding* often sound as if they are trying to achieve the same effect with the language: they force it into a new mold, streamline it, give it *cachet.* They make it into a machine with a minimum of moving parts, but with constant *upgrades* and (naturally) *enhancements.* And if you want to get reconciliation taken seriously, you had better put your case in these terms. The politician's imitation of the style is a remote sign of the gathering belief that the whole world—or such parts of it that function properly—can be understood either as a metaphor for free market economics and the management philosophies it has spawned or as an actual consequence of them. That is to say, as an *outcome* or an *event*.

Many things that in the past simply happened now happen as *events* or *episodes*. *Events* are to the natural world what *outcomes* are to the man-made—and like *outcomes,* they must be managed. When the Meteorology Office predicts *weather* or *rain* in Australia, they are now inclined to add *event* to it. They will say, "There has not been a *rain event* in the northwest since February, but there have been a couple of *weather events* on the eastern slopes." In the present climate Gene Kelly would sing "Singin' in the Rain Event" and Billie Holiday "Stormy Weather Event." In the United States they speak not only of weather *events* but *debris events*. Americans witnessed several *debris events* as the *Challenger* returned to earth. Landslides and floods are *debris events*. Hardly a day goes by without one.

We may be thankful that nature does not easily give in to the new language: in a leaflet telling customers that their supply was about to be turned off, Sydney Water recently advised that *times may vary depending upon the nature of the encounter problems associated with bad weather*. Rarely in history have sensible human beings found it so hard to say simple things.

Primo Levi was right: people who write and speak like this cannot be happy. It is said that a happy worker is a good worker, and what workers would not be happier if the sentences they wrote and read were less like clogged drains? What if they were more like babbling brooks? If they were clear and yet contained an image or two and a bit of fun or verve or had a sinew of imagination like this sentence from the page in Faulkner quoted earlier: *Back running, tunneled between the two sets of bobbing mule ears, the road vanishes beneath the wagon as though it were a ribbon and the front axle were a spool?* If that's too fanciful, what if we aimed to make it simple, as simple as *Go wash them hands,* which appears on the same page of Faulkner? What's hard about that? There is no need to *implement* anything or *strategize* about it, and no one ever says *in terms of the bathroom,* or *in respect of the bathroom, you should wash your hands in it.* No one says *Hopefully we can have your commitment to a scenario in terms of the truck which will have you in place in it within a reasonable timeframe, Rover.* We say, *Get in,* and Rover gets in. But the public language, which could easily stimulate our minds and have an effect like music on our souls, is drowning us in sludge.

Being adapted to its quarry—the profound, uncertain, elusive truth—language is often tentative. Much of the phrasing in truth-seeking language, including poetry, is provisional. Arguments and stories are built on blocks or in layers, like an oil painting. The plots of novels, the truth of poems (like life), turn on minute variations, nuance, an impulse, chance, a shade of meaning. But in politics—and in marketing—the pressure is away from the provisional and toward the absolute. This is to say, away from reality.

Yes or no are not the only honest answers in a complex, transitional world. But in politics and business they are demanded. The language that evolves is squeezed out of this contradiction: the demand to be categorical and the necessity (and the instinct) to hedge. True, there are plenty of downright lies and deliberate half-truths. But there are, as well, attempts to answer questions that, politically speaking, are unanswerable.

Weasel words are no less the product of their environment than weasels are. In the diabolical environment of politics, unreasoning forces throw up unreasoning things like red herrings and dead cats, and fling them in the path of journalists. Politicians come forth willing to say almost anything, frequently without regard to ordinary civility. Their opponents are rank hypocrites, they say: they have secret plans that all the outward signs disguise. And often it emerges that these outrageous accusations have some truth to them, because politics does throw up hypocrites and liars. In keeping with the evolution of such political animals, among journalists horrible cynics emerge.

In this contest the language becomes the agent of a whole climate of deceit. Spin abounds. Whatever is most hackneyed triumphs over anything informative or fresh. Whatever suits the story. Syntax is mangled. Reason goes up in smoke. The truth is less significant than the political contest. The question is not *Which is the better argument?* It is *Who won?* Or *What was the outcome?* With reason and enlightenment, the language goes out the window, and with them go many opportunities for humor, spontaneity, originality, and surprise. When did you last hear or see a politician to whom any of these words conspicuously apply?

Television news purports to tell us what is going on in the world. It tells us, however, in much the same way that the word "cookies" written on a cookie package, or "gorilla" written on a gorilla cage, tells us about cookies and gorillas. News on TV is not much more than *signage*—the current word for more than one sign, as in "God sent Moses a piece of *signage*" or "Moses had a *signage event* that *empowered* him *going forward*." Naturally the TV news cannot tell us everything, but it is the principal medium of information for the masses, the crucial medium of government and politics—and, of course, the sleekest of vehicles for marketing.

TV news is delivered from a certain elevation, and like it or not must be taken seriously by everyone who relies on public opinion. Politicians, businesspeople, sports people, people with a story to tell, along with the journalists themselves, bring to the daily news prefabricated news grabs and all-purpose platitudes. If we are kind, we might forgive them all on the Machiavellian basis that this is their job— or their media manager's—and the only sin is doing it badly. To give their stories a chance of going seamlessly into the world, government (and company) press releases have long been written in the language of the newspapers and electronic media: they offer a headline, an opening paragraph, and a quote, and they hope that the media will run with it as if they wrote it themselves. So the language of the media and the language of politics and business are blended. If one is a peculiar, dishonest, or debased language, the other is bound to become so.

In the media, sound bites grow ever shorter and more tendentious even if this also means they are misleading, inadequate, or silly. TV news adopts a strange sentence structure to accompany images. It is, after all, a visual medium.

When the technology for sound arrived, the old film directors did not take long in deciding: where words and images compete, go with the image. It's the image they'll remember the next day, and the next week and possibly for the rest of their lives. Television reportage is weighted in the same way. The words over the image sound remote, staccato, disembodied. They serve as an almost subliminal support to the pictures. A school fire in January 2003 is reported: *Two hundred staff rallied together, some needing counseling, later inspecting the devastation firsthand.* The sentence has been stitched together to match fleeting pictures of people in a meeting room, a person standing, a burned building. And then the reporter eyeballs us and says: *It's been described as a phoenix rising from the ashes. . . .* Thus another suburban drama has been turned into a soap.

There is no solution to this, nothing at least that might be called *structural*. It's in the nature of the medium, and the medium is essentially one for marketing. After that, it's a medium for entertainment. Information and the public interest do not exactly come third, but, rather, have to fight for a place among the advertising and jokes. The principles of marketing are not the same as the principles of democracy. The first principle of marketing, according to some schools, is to "turn wants into needs." Whatever we take that to mean, it is probably not what most of us expect from our political system. But we are talking principles: talk realities and we begin to find common ground.

Marketing asserts, first, the right to choice and, second, the right to manipulate us by any means short of extortion and blackmail into believing that there is no choice but to buy a particular product. This as well is not an axiom that most of us would think particularly desirable in politics. But while many of us would not see the ambitions of democracy and the ambitions of marketing as the same, we are sure to recognize similarities between such marketing ambitions and democratic practice. The language is bound to express this overlap.

Those old filmmakers were right, of course. Pictures rule. To the extent that TV rules, pictures rule; and to the extent that TV is the most important medium of public life, the public language is at best a secondary consideration and at worst indistinguishable from the language of marketing and entertainment. No wonder, then, that political parties become *poll driven,* that their political strategies are essentially marketing strategies built on the same kinds of demographic research and replete with the same kinds of slogans and messages. No wonder that the trend in politics is increasingly toward sending messages, sometimes subliminally, to the increasingly narrow sections of the population that are reckoned to count politically. For the rest, governing the country seems to have been transformed, in Joan Didion's words, "into a series of signals meant for someone else."

The great screenwriter Jean-Claude Carrière says, "A film is complete when the screenplay is vanished." So maybe the language suffers a slow death as the world becomes more like a film, or one at least that we understand as much through images as words. Is this what Australian Prime Minister John Howard understood when he went to Bali after the bombs exploded? He was seen embracing the victims, grieving with them, and it must have been that people were comforted by these images, because his approval ratings rose. Yet he spoke no notable words.

Likewise, although he was within easy helicopter range, President Bush announced victory in Iraq by arriving on the aircraft carrier *Abraham Lincoln* in a Viking jet. He wore full military attire, which was something President Eisenhower, an actual general, and President Kennedy, an actual war hero, never did. Nothing Bush said had a hope of matching the drama of the pictures. We can safely presume that nothing was intended to.

There were words on the *Abraham Lincoln*: the words were "Mission accomplished," and they were, of course, horribly misleading if not a full-blown lie. But they were words for the media moment, an advertising slogan, and no one really expects advertising slogans to be truthful. More recently the White House released a memo from Condoleezza ("Condi") Rice telling the president "Iraq is sovereign," and the president's spontaneous scrawl on it, "Let freedom reign" (which he might have plagiarized from Martin Luther King). The words and the document were surely concocted to simulate a "historic document," an image for the front pages of newspapers and for television, a dramatic context for the words.

Pictures rule, but words define, explain, express, direct, and hold together our thoughts and what we know. They lead us into new ideas and back to older ones. In the beginning was the Word. It might help everyone a little if among the *signage* in the newsroom—or the party room, or any room where decisions that concern a nation's life are made—there was one that quoted the writer Barry Lopez: "Take care for the spiritual quality, the holy quality, the serious quality of the language."

•

CHAPTER 3

THE POST-TRUTH
ENVIRONMENT

•

"Don't you see that the whole aim of Newspeak is to narrow the range of thought?"
—GEORGE ORWELL, *1984*

•

"The vaguely quantitative words 'significant' and 'significantly' are used five times on this slide with de facto meanings ranging from detectable in a largely irrelevant calibration case study, to an amount of damage so that everyone dies, to a difference of six-hundred-forty-fold."
—EDWARD R. TUFTE ON THE COLUMBIA SPACE SHUTTLE DEBRIS ASSESSMENT TEAM'S POWERPOINT PRESENTATION

•

"We need to counter the shock wave of the evil-doer by having individual rate cuts accelerated and by thinking about tax rebates."
—GEORGE W. BUSH

•

"Who could not be moved by the sight of that poor, demoralized rabble, outwitted, outflanked, outmaneuvered by the U.S. military? Yet, given time, I think the press will bounce back."
—JAMES BAKER, QUOTED IN THE *GUARDIAN,* MARCH 1991

•

"Calibrate me, Dick . . . Dick, calibrate me, if I'm wrong."
—DONALD RUMSFELD, 2004

•

"The true hypocrite is the one who ceases to perceive his deception, the one who lies with sincerity."
—ANDRÉ GIDE

•

I N THE AFTERMATH OF AL QAEDA'S ATTACK ON NEW YORK and Washington, Philip Roth told *Le Figaro*: "Language is always a lie, above all public language." He seemed to be saying that as the volume of public language had been greater since 9/11, so had the volume of lies. He might also have observed that never has the language so lacked the capacity to utter truth. Those who spoke and wrote the public language in the past often lacked the motivation to say honestly what they meant, but now they seem to lack the words as well. When George W. Bush speaks, all Philip Roth hears, he says, are the voices of ventriloquists.

Philip Roth is not the only one to imagine a ventriloquist's hand up George W. Bush's shirt. We all pretty well take it for granted that our leaders are either scripted or in other ways programmed by their advisers. Only some of us mind, and even then we're often inclined to think that the ventriloquists might make more sense than the people we elected. And the ventriloquists make them say things we want to hear. Say *jobs,* they tell them before they go out to meet the media: say *growth,* say *evil,* say *liberal,* say *women,* say *strong,* say *humble*—say *strong but humble.* And they say them. And because they have been market-researched, they comfort us as familiar things comfort us, as clichés comfort us. *Strong but humble*: sounds good to me, we say. Can't get enough of it, we say. Amen.

To be *strong but humble* is a mantra of modern business leadership. The idea did not begin with *managerialism,* but it is possible that the U.S. president or one of his advisers picked it up in business school. No American administration has ever contained so many CEOs. In the presidential debates during his first U.S. election campaign, George W. Bush recommended being strong, but he also said, "Ours will be a humble nation." Almost everything that has happened since winning that election renders this statement a hoax equivalent to the Australian prime minister's "I will never, ever introduce a Goods and Service Tax." The Australian prime minister imposed such a tax as soon as he had won an election by saying he wouldn't. The U.S. president's pledge of humility was no less misleading, and we may reasonably assume that it was no more sincere. This is why speakers of the public language should be pursued relentlessly, not only for the facts they aver and the thoughts they profess, but for the words they use. Someone should have asked the Australian PM if his words meant that he would resign before he went back on them. And someone should have asked the presidential candidate what he meant by "humble": what "humble" meant to him and what signs of it we should look for in his administration.

Our leaders in Washington are forever invoking him, so

let's go back to Lincoln and his Gettysburg Address. Or to Pericles' address to the Athenians during the Peloponnesian Wars. Here are two famous examples of public language. Made more than two thousand years apart, both memorialize those who died in battle, both seek meaning in their deaths. They can still persuade us that every word is true. Here is Pericles (or at least what Thucydides recalled of it):

> What their eyes showed plainly must be done they trusted their own valor to accomplish, thinking it more glorious to defend themselves and die in the attempt than to yield and live. From the reproach of cowardice, indeed, they fled, but presented their bodies to the shock of battle; when insensible of fear, but triumphing in hope, in the doubtful charge they instantly dropped— and thus discharged the duty which brave men own owed their country.

We can tell that Pericles did not show his speech to any firm of political or business consultants, or a team of ministerial advisers, because he has described the soldiers' deaths without saying they were *committed* or *showed commitment*. There is no *hopefully* in it. They did not seek, according to Pericles at least, any *enhancement* of their reputations. They saw duty as owed their country, not *in terms of* it. The sentences are full of verbs, empty of cliché and airy euphemisms. The dead are not the *fallen*. Death is death and not an *outcome*. There is no *closure*. In our world you might think that life is not worth living without *closure*.

And here is Lincoln, also verb-filled, in what William Safire called "the best short speech since the Sermon on the Mount," at Gettysburg after the battle in 1863:

Four score and seven years ago our fathers brought forth on this continent, a new nation, conceived in liberty, and dedicated to the proposition that all men are created equal. Now we are engaged in a great civil war, testing whether that nation, or any nation so conceived and so dedicated, can long endure. We are met on a great battlefield of that war. We have come to dedicate a portion of that field, as a final resting place for those who here gave their lives that that nation might live. It is altogether fitting and proper that we should do this. But in a larger sense, we cannot dedicate—we cannot consecrate—we cannot hallow—this ground. The brave men, living and dead, who struggled here, have consecrated it, far above our poor power to add or detract. The world will little note, nor long remember, what we say here, but it can never forget what they did here. . . .

Not so: as it turned out, the speech outlived the deed. But one brave verb keeps the deed alive: "struggled." He might have chosen from a dozen clichés or dressed it up with an adverb (*heroically, manfully, gallantly*). Instead, like Pericles' soldiers presenting "their bodies to the shock of battle," Lincoln chose a word that reaches into the imagination and flicks a little switch that illuminates the truth for us. "What they did here" is contained in that word "struggled." Read aloud, it can make you shudder. This is what is meant by the power of words.

There is another famous example of public language, also commemorating the fallen, hardly less powerful and also a wonder of rhetoric: the speech Shakespeare gave Mark Antony at Julius Caesar's funeral.

Friends, Romans, countrymen, lend me your ears;
I come to bury Caesar, not to praise him.
The evil that men do lives after them;
The good is oft interred with their bones.

But Antony's speech, while much like the other two, is also very different. Among other things. it is an early example of political spin: he puts a spin on Caesar's death, or, rather, a counterspin to the assassins' actions and especially to Brutus: "For Brutus is an honorable man" and "I am no orator, as Brutus is":

But were I Brutus,
And Brutus Antony, there were an Antony
Would ruffle up your spirits, and put a tongue
In every wound of Caesar, that should move
The stones of Rome to rise and mutiny.

In Antony's speech we have a Roman (or Elizabethan) prototype for *dog whistling*—the name now given to the trick of tapping the political potential of suppressed prejudice, fear, and envy through apparently harmless but carefully "coded" words, and turning it against the rest of the country. Antony knows "the power of speech to stir men's blood" and his speech, to use his own word, is intended to do "mischief." His words ring true but conceal the truth of his real purpose.

We are used to this. The constant fog of lies and half-lies, filtered truth, information, misinformation, disinformation— spin and counterspin—is endemic to the information age. We live in a "post-truth environment," to borrow Eric Alterman's phrase. Yet we are not the first citizens of a democracy to live with spin and calculated lies. The Greeks wrote voluminously on the subject of rhetoric and its potential for both good and evil works. "I will give him soft talk," Medea says before she lays the direst of all traps for Jason. We've been trying to tell the difference between soft talk and hard truth ever since. George Orwell recognized the signs half a century ago. In 1939 the French filmmaker Jean Renoir saw himself living at a time when "everyone lies; governments, radios, movies, newspapers." He was right beyond doubt, and he was far from the only one to notice. The lies are just as pervasive and oppressive now, and take ever more ingenious forms.

Joined to a brilliant understanding of their hearts and minds, Antony's words bring the mob to mistake his ambition for a noble cause. Indeed he *ennobles* them—though today we would make do with *empowers*. Whatever it is he does to them, he also serves himself in doing it. And every time we hear a politician speak, a fight breaks out between our need to believe and our instinct to distrust. The struggle is because the power of words, as the Czech playwright and former president Václav Havel said a decade ago,

> is neither immediate nor clear-cut. . . . Words that electrify society with their freedom and truthfulness are matched by words that mesmerize, deceive, inflame, madden. . . . The selfsame word can at one time be the cornerstone of peace, while at another, machine-gun fire resounds in its every syllable.

By way of example we might compare the U.S. president's address to the Congress after September 11 with a speech made by Boris Yeltsin after the attempted coup in

Moscow in 1991. The Bush speech had some resoundingly good lines, but it was also debilitated by cliché and a tone of Hollywood vengeance. It was, moreover, too plainly stitched together by other hands. No doubt it moved many Americans. But a fragment of Yeltsin's little speech has a more universal power. Addressing directly the parents of three young men who died defending their new freedom, he said: "Forgive me, your president, that I could not defend, could not save your sons." Words can bestow nobility on both those who speak them and those about whom they are spoken. They can do this even if they are not literally true or the speaker is not widely regarded as a noble person. They can make us surrender, of themselves.

In particular, words do this when they break free of the speaker's narcissism and express an understanding of another's feelings and point of view, where the words are "thoughts charged with emotion" and the thoughts are more than platitudes and the emotion is more than the speaker's.

In Colonel Tim Collins's "We go to liberate, not to conquer" address to his British troops in Iraq, the thoughts are clear and uncompromised. He does not call on God for help or justification. He speaks of wiping out the enemy, of being "ferocious" in battle. He confronts death on both sides squarely. His thoughts are the more powerful because he also speaks with understanding of the Iraqi people and their history. And more powerful still because the words are spontaneous. They sound like the words of a military commander, whereas the words of President Bush on the *Abraham Lincoln* sound like the words of a politician dressed up as a military commander. No political leader among the coalition countries managed rhetoric that came close to

Collins's extemporaneous address, including Tony Blair, who is always eloquent but never quite escapes the politician's tone of nagging self-justification.

It may be mischief, but Antony's is stirring, memorable mischief, mischief made by someone who respects and knows the powers of language. For the most part, our own leaders are less eloquent, less than Shakespeare, naturally enough, and less than Havel, but also less eloquent than not-so-long-ago leaders had to be. Eloquence is no guarantee of truth. Antony's speech is one proof of that. There are countless others. During and long after the World War I the public language was invaded by grotesque euphemisms for pointless and outrageous death and mutilation. Those words that Hemingway called obscenities were contained in perfectly constructed sentences. They still appear at ceremonies commemorating the 1918 armistice. Anything rather than speak of death and the chance of meaninglessness. But eloquence gives truth a chance. For Aristotle, rhetoric was a dangerous weapon but one that truth must take up or be defeated.

Now, through the media, our leaders have learned, or at least their advisers have, that they still have the power "to stir men's blood," but by less-articulate means—with mantras, a well-placed platitude on the radio, a bit of cant tossed lightly to a press pack, a gesture on TV. All these will do as well as any speech to conceal the truth or hold the populace in thrall. Perhaps after the twin towers and the Bali bombing, nothing adequate could be said. Perhaps that old line about words being inadequate at times like this is more than a banality. However, it is more likely that the absence of memorable words to make some sense of these tragedies was a sign that our politicians reckon that words are inferior to images, especially images of grieving with the families of the victims. It is a symptom of language's declining status, and you can see the same symptoms at pretty well any funeral—or wedding, or board meeting.

•

Political terminology is never adequate to the multitudinous reality it seeks to define. Likewise, political leaders, staring down forests of microphones and lenses while journalists quiz them about that reality, invariably lack the inhuman skill to give answers that are both definitive and truthful. They develop other skills instead. They learn to say: "We are *committed* to this, yes, at this point in time, absolutely, Michelle." Politics is a wrestling match with chaos, and it prizes those who seem best able to impose their will upon the impossible. Successful politicians are those who can conjure up an image of things that approximates the view from where the rest of us are standing. The best of them do this by changing our view to theirs. The hacks seek out our view and try to make it their own.

In the 1980s, governments throughout the Western world made the reality economic. People who stepped outside were declared exiled, feral, or wet. Or dinosaurs, socialists, or bleeding hearts. In all events, they were said to be *unreconstructed,* and they were sent to play in the minor leagues or forced into early retirement. This was the political dimension of the phrase *the main game.* The main game was the *agenda,* and the people who *set the agenda* or *owned the agenda* mocked all other agendas and warned of calamity should these alternative agendas ever become reality.

Every time a government sets an agenda, it sets the language. The *economic rationalist* or *supply side* or *monetarist* or

free market or *liberal* or *liberalized* (the terms are not as precise as they sound) agenda of the 1980s brought forth scores
of new terms hitherto known only to a few economists and
bureaucrats. Suddenly politicians began spouting them,
and they recruited to their teams economists and businesspeople who fed them with yet more new words and, so that
they might sound convincing at news conferences, coached
them in pronunciation and the relationships between one
term and another. When the politicians were found wanting, a new breed of economic curmudgeon came forth.
Until then only a few superstars like John Maynard Keynes
or J. K. Galbraith had managed to make themselves widely
known in society, but now that there was no such thing as
society—only an economy or a market—economists
emerged like rats from the cupboards in which they had
been properly kept for generations. They found media slots,
grew personalities, and began telling us in terms we'd never
heard before that if we did not change our ways, we'd end
up like Argentina. They formed "think tanks," and these
think tanks began to set the agenda for the political parties.
The think tanks produced scholarly economic papers and
fed them to like-minded economists with newspaper
columns. The newspaper columnists would tell the public
or *warn the government* that the economic indicators were
painting an alarming picture of a nation in decline. Argentina
might be mentioned as a *worst-case scenario.* And if we did
nothing to *enhance our competitiveness,* even the *best-case scenario* would be much worse than Japan. (The Japanese economy, you will recall, was the *paradigm* in those days, but
since then there has been a *paradigm shift* and no one really
talks about it anymore.)

Some of the politicians became very good at the new

economic language. They had to be or they wouldn't get a spot in the Cabinet. Indeed, anyone who wanted to get on in life, or just to be taken seriously, had to be sufficiently fluent in economic language to talk convincingly about the *current account* and the *current account deficit* or *CAD*. An Australian treasurer revealed at a press conference that he didn't know what *GOS* stood for. Too late, a journalist told him it was the *Gross Operating Share*: the prime minister sacked him that afternoon.

No one has heard of the GOS for a decade. It seems to have gone away, perhaps to Argentina. For that matter, no one seems much concerned by the CAD anymore; but in those days even ordinary people (this was before they became *customers*) who for most of their lives had had nothing better to worry about than their health or the education of their children or world poverty or nuclear annihilation learned that the CAD was a devilish thing, and if they weren't worrying about it, and wondering how the nation might best *leverage its comparative advantage,* they were living in a fool's paradise.

It's all past now. No one asks what *supply-side economics* is—they just do it. Politicians no longer whip themselves into moral furies about monetary policy—it's a *no-brainer*. R. J. Hawke, the Australian prime minister who sacked the illiterate treasurer, no longer berates his people or the language. Australians miss him as, no doubt, old Bolsheviks missed Lenin. Lenin was said to have almost miraculous powers of oratory. "When Trotsky spoke we listened: when Lenin spoke we marched," an old comrade is reported to have said. When Hawke spoke we marveled; and grammarians positively trembled. Hawke was one of those politicians for whom it sometimes seemed words were less the medium of expression than just so many bloody obstacles placed in the way of people who needed to see what he bloody saw. When speaking off the cuff, he embarked on his sentences like a madman with a club in a dark room: he bumped and crashed around so long, his listeners became less interested in what he was saying than the prospect of his escape. He would say there were "three things to consider, and in respect of the first, which is the obvious need for fiscal tightening in respect of the budgetary situation which in terms of a surplus you don't need to be a rocket scientist to see is at this point in time a deficit . . ." And so it would go on.

When at last he emerged triumphant into the light, we cheered, not for the gift of enlightenment but as we cheer a man who walks away from an avalanche or mining accident. And Mr. Hawke would raise his tremendous eyebrow as if to say "Now you see, for I have told you." His glittering career—like those of presidents Bush and Reagan—was proof that *in respect of* modern political success, political leaders do not need to be masterly—or even competent—with words.

What they do need is an agenda they can "own." Crime, taxation, family values, national security, and the flaws in your opponent's character are perennial agendas. Only the owners change, and ownership is always achieved with a slogan, or a gesture, or a look; a certain something including war service; a posture determined not by argument, principle, or even eloquence but by opinion polls and the party's marketing strategy.

All successful politicians must be at least competent in the first part of Aristotelian dialectics, which is to rebut their opponents' case and persuasively put their own. But success depends on persuading the judge, or at least it did until the skills of modern marketing and research made it possible to second-guess the judge—which is to say, the people—instead. Inevitably, the rhetorical skills grow weaker as the market research grows stronger. Success is not determined in the parliament but in the polling—and on the television. It's decided very largely by how often we judges hear the words we want to hear. When we hear them, and confirm them, not with our vote, but our voting *intention,* the words become sacrosanct. They become the narrative, the *story.* The *story* says this is how we got here (by economic reform, or by sacrifice, or *by the values* of the *frontier,* or *community,* or by willingness to undertake adventures), so this is what matters. Those who do not know or respect the story—or the *paradigm*—must live outside the tribe. It is not Nazi Germany, but it doesn't always feel like democracy when the only reality seems to be that of the ruling group.

The difference between a dictatorship and a poll-driven democracy is that dictators kill or incarcerate their own citizens for political reasons. Dictatorships will not stand doubt: propaganda is used to create certainty, with terror in reserve. Democracies don't do this. But the language of modern democratic politics is increasingly ruthless toward doubters, or even people with imagination. Parties stay *on strategy,* leaders *on message,* and the *message* and the *strategy* are both drawn from the polls, which means that anyone who thinks differently may be interpreted as resisting the will of the people. The language is constructed so that it never leads the mind to those places minds naturally go—toward mysteries, contradictions, multitudes.

What makes democracies different, governments and

the media would have us believe, is *balance*. A spread of opinions—pro and con; right and left; Conservative and progressive, oddballs and obsessives in proportion. Privately owned media regulate their own balance: balance in public broadcasting is usually a mixture of self-regulation, statutory obligations, and government coercion. Balanced opinions, or a balance of opinions, are in general better than a lack of balance. But balance is not in itself principle, truth, reason, or fairness. It does not mean "the right judgment," though a politician who says that he decided to increase taxation, abolish pensions, or invade another country *on balance* might want you to believe that it does. It's not the balance; it's the judgment. Chamberlain's *on balance* judgment at Munich was the wrong one. Sometimes courage and instinct are at least as important as balance, and necessary to determine what it is that must be balanced. Balance is useless without knowledge, insight, and conviction; it can even be invoked to curb the exercise of those faculties.

Yet balance is presented to us as if it were essential to all understanding. Believing that balance will grant us wisdom, we might as well believe that where balance exists, political spin cannot work: or muckraking, name-calling, stonewalling, wedge politics, dog whistling, slogans, or weasel words. But these techniques were invented for a system where balance prevails, to exploit and manipulate us behind its curtain. We should view *balance* with the suspicion we reserve for any word used repeatedly in public affairs. As with a word like "choice" in marketing, it is not that balance is less than desirable in democracy, but rather that too much is claimed with it and too often. It has become a weasel word.

But cliché describes it just as well. Or even "lie." Balance, which is essential to the law, to argument, to nature, and to democracy, is also one of those words that have been co-opted to serve a purpose at odds with their accepted meaning. It is the kind of cliché that "organizes life," to borrow Václav Havel's words: "it expropriates people's identity; it becomes ruler, defense lawyer, judge and the law."

Modern political language has this much in common with propaganda. And something in common with war, which, like politics, is conducted according to *strategies*. As with defense forces (or bureaucracies—wherever careers are carved out), political practitioners are prone to believe their own bullshit. Words and phrases that began life as convenient catchalls for complex and various phenomena become indisputable truth, the last word in human understanding. Inadequate or ridiculous words are made into mantras that no one in politics can resist. Consider the word "aspirational." *Aspirational* voters, we are told, are voters who want a better life for themselves and for their children. And we wonder if we ever met someone who wanted a worse life. *Aspirationals* are distinguished by their desire to get on in life. They aspire to ownership: a home, a share portfolio, a holiday house, a good education for their children. And we wonder if the same was not true of our own generation, and our parents' and grandparents' generations, and if these *aspirationals* are different from anyone who ever tasted hope.

In the end we see that the word "aspirational" derives not from any distinguishing aspirations but from the numbers of them. It is this that gives them political—and commercial—importance. Otherwise we might ask why someone who aspires to the elite is admirable while members of the elite are despised. Why is the desire for a non–business-related SUV laudable if not heroic, while ownership of such a vehicle proves your membership of a parasitic class? For that matter, how do *aspirationals* differ from social climbers, wannabes, and philistines, who in other times have been scorned? The 1920s was an era of *aspirationals,* and look what happened. The answer is that politicians can't get elected without them. Their votes count for more than any elite's. That is the *bottom line* about *aspirationals* in politics, as it is for those who sell the things to which they aspire. In that word the merger of politics and marketing is completed. And the longer you look at it, the more you wonder if the decline of language and the decline of history are not material aids to both the merger and the progress of stupidity.

Political and corporate thinking have merged in this development. On both sides the fashion is for *strategies* and *outcomes.* The latter is a modern portmanteau to hold such words as "result," "consequence," "upshot," "product," "effect," "return," and "happenstance," which are all subtly different and don't suggest, as "outcome" does, that everything in the world is or can be governed by *strategies.* Without *outcomes* you can't have *accountability,* another catch-all to replace more challenging concepts like integrity, honesty, decency, truth, and justice. *Accountability* makes people with the capacity to do good fear for the consequences of doing something for which they might be held accountable. So long as it runs on the principle of *accountability,* a business or department is less likely to profess, practice, or even know anything about imagination, courage, initiative, reflection, or generosity (to name just a few), which have been priceless human qualities until now and great aids to getting at the truth. It is even possible that the fashion for *accountability* encourages the use of dead words—because what is dead contains no threat.

The sibling of "accountability" is "transparency," which in the new language is intended to denote that the public is able to see what's going on. You will see it in the financial pages; it crops up regularly in Parliament and other places where the public language is spoken. Companies and government departments frequently include it in their mission statements. In most cases they are *committed* to it. *Transparency* is desirable, but when you see the word so often, you can't help wondering if it's not hiding something. There must be other words to describe what amounts to no more than a mere arrangement to enable public scrutiny, even if it's only a *commitment* to it.

More words can be found for the moral and ethical matters involved, more words for questions of interest and motivation, and more still, if business ever got down to it, for matters of self-knowledge and self-discipline. In this instance, as in so many others, the depletion of the language actually depletes our capacity to judge, to argue, to identify possibility. This includes the possibility that the new words are worse than useless if everyone—the honest, the dishonest, and the undecided—can say with equal sincerity, as they do, that they are *committed* to them. BAE Systems says it is committed to "ensure" that our "CSR [Corporate Social Responsibility] activities are fully aligned with our efforts to deliver our key business objectives," as if aligning your "five guiding values" with the guided missiles you make and sell solves all your ethical problems—even when the first of your "five guiding values" is to "delight all [your] . . . customers." Titan Corporation says that it has a "reputation for excellence and commitment to upholding the highest ethical standards." "All of Titan's employees share certain core values." Likewise, at CACI, the first of their Ten Values is "Placing integrity and honesty above all else" and the second is "Putting clients first." We must presume that any contradiction between the first and second values will be resolved by "aligning" them. Catchwords like these—alignment, commitment, values—are no longer living "words," but more akin to minor deities or icons whose meaning has long been forgotten or never understood.

The organization (or cult) ritually pays obeisance and goes back to its *core business*. Much the same can be said of most (*key*) words in mission statements. If a drawing of a toad were substituted for *accountability,* and a carving of the Egyptian goddess Sekhmet were placed in a corner for *transparency,* and once a year everyone renewed their *commitments* to them, nothing material would change.

There may be a connection between believing in these business terms and the widespread sense of *entitlement* that Robert Hughes, among others, has observed in our society. Some medical scientists tell us that the two most significant changes in medicine in the past century were first, scientific development, and second, the growing belief that no mistake, inadequacy, and failure should be accepted as a normal part of life. Now many of our fellow citizens, especially those in the United States—oddly, for people who believe in a Great Disposer—believe that some human agency or process is to blame for every inconvenient twist of fortune. Without blame, there cannot be *closure,* and there cannot be *closure* without litigation or litigation without *closure.*

By radically reducing the element of chance in life, science is chiefly responsible for this development. But the language of modern marketing and management might be adding to the trend. With all the talk of *outcomes* and *events* and *accountability* and such, it could be that these days many citizens are prone to think that most *events* are managed, and that those that aren't should be: managed *transparently,* in fact, into *agreed outcomes.* And if there is no such *outcome,* someone must be made *accountable.* There must be *closure.* It is very likely that the word creates the need. The most dramatic example so far appears to be the news that in some parts of the United States parents have started legal proceedings against their obstetricians when, on reaching high school age, their children's IQs do not meet expectations.

It is odd that modern conservatives, who make so much of our cultural heritage, make very little of its single most important element, the language. The Australian prime minister, whose worldview is largely informed by what he takes to be English conservative tradition, is not informed in any way that his constituents can enjoy by the English language. By his own reckoning, John Howard is the most conservative of Australian leaders; yet he is also the most modern in that platitudes are pretty well all he attempts. Every Australia Day, every Anzac Day, and every day of disaster he pulls out the old Australian *mateship* nostrum. The idea that mateship is a defining Australian characteristic emerged from the literature of the rural frontier and the first World War. Its literal meaning is friendship and loyalty between men. Mr. Howard tells his fellow Australians that *mateship* is what defines them, as if it is *all* that defines them, all they need to know about themselves, and all that he can think to say about them. In truth this *is* all he needs to say; it is the verbal equivalent of a physical gesture: a wave, a handshake, a wink, a nod. It will do for the occasion.

The godfather of conservatives, Edmund Burke, once said, "Magnanimity in politics is not seldom the truest wisdom; a great empire and little minds go ill together." A lack of Burkean intelligence or magnanimity might be one reason why political leaders no longer reach such memorable conclusions. Another reason is the absence of an audience for them. Modern politics is a media narrative, and the last thing you need is philosophy getting in the way of it. The words that count are those that feed the story. Advisers are employed for these story-concocting skills, and speech-writers generally take their orders from them. Such gems of reflective prose as might occasionally be crafted make it into public life only when judged *on message,* or not too far off it. This means that we scarcely ever hear one. In fact, insisting that leaders stay *on message* is different only in degree from any Ministry of Propaganda dictum.

The language of our political leaders rarely steps far from the ordinary for the good reason that ordinary language is what people use. Very likely they also calculate that underlying the sound of ordinariness is the message of common sense, which to a literal mind means the sense of common people. From this, rather than any obvious signs of thought, modern political language gets its gravity. It is assumed that a man who speaks the language of the people will embody their wisdom. And so long as polls and elections go the way of a leader, there will be plenty of commentators to say that he is tuned in to the people and is much deeper than he sounds.

Sometimes our leaders are indeed tuned in and sometimes it is mere illusion. Tony Blair was tuned in when, as Britons heard that Princess Diana was dead, he stepped forth to call her "the people's Princess." That he was dressed in jeans for the occasion was even more tuned in. But not every political leader can wear jeans. The Australian prime minister frequently tunes in to the people while wearing power-walking gear. American presidents go for hats and say things like "We're comin' after 'em" and go back to their golf, as if a golf club were a surrogate laser-guided missile and anything in its path a terrorist or varmint.

To be sure, it is good to be tuned in. It is a comfort to some, a source of amusement to others. It provides work for semioticians. But it's slumming it. Being in tune with the people and using what is taken to be their language is not the same thing as thinking, or being honest.

Compare being tuned in with Burke, whose power of thought cannot be separated from the prose in which he expresses it. In fact, we cannot be sure where the thought ends and the words begin. We will never know if Burke arrived at his maxim about little minds and large empires before he wrote the sentence or in the writing of it. We do know, however, that with writing, it is sometimes one way and sometimes the other. Such wisdom as we have, we express in language, and in language we also seek wisdom. An impoverished language must perforce accompany impoverished thought. As Orwell said: "It becomes ugly and inaccurate because our thoughts are foolish, but the slovenliness of our language makes it easier for us to have foolish thoughts."

Here is the Australian prime minister again, and remember, this is not off the top of his head but has been composed to enlighten his fellow Australians about the war on terror:

Australians respect and understand the many cultures and religions that make up our society. Now, more than ever, we must work together to make sure no religion or section of our community is made to feel a scapegoat because of the actions of a small number of fanatics.

This confection touches neither the heart nor the head, and gives no sign of coming from either of those places. It's a comforter, as dead things are for some people. Lifelessness, however, does not entirely disguise the little sleights of hand. Look closely and you'll see that the corpse has been tampered with. No one must be made to *feel* a scapegoat. Some people (Edmund Burke, for example) might have expected him to say that no one should be *made* a scapegoat. It might be an unintended slip, of course, but it sends the message—it's all right to blame them, but don't let them hear you.

At another point the Australian prime minister says: "As a people we have traditionally engaged the world optimistically." And while he's rolling on this theme: "Our open, friendly nature makes us welcome guests and warm hosts." This rose-colored boasting smells of some nightmare Ministry of Information. In the diary he kept through the Nazi years, Viktor Klemperer recorded the same tone in the German public language. To establish as fact the myth of German superiority, the Third Reich's propagandists pursued two mutually reinforcing themes: the inferiority of certain others and the delightfulness of themselves.

As a people, the Germans were *culture loving, nature loving, fun loving* and *peace loving*. The German nation and the German people were always *young. Sunny,* Klemperer says, was a favorite term, especially in birth and funeral notices. *As a people,* the Germans also had an *irrepressible will,* and so on. This *will* was set in direct opposition to *elites* and intellectuals of any kind. *Elites* were not *useful*. This idealistic portrait of *sunny* German folk was matched, of course, by equally absurd depictions of Jews, Slavs, Bolsheviks, and others—and soon the German language, like the Nazi regime, was rotten to its roots. We need not fear a new

Third Reich in our democracies, but that is all the more reason for not adopting its tones.

The phrase *as a people* might not be a lie, but it smells like one. And it sits askew to the element of conservative political philosophy that opposes all attempts to categorize people by class or historic tendency, or any other conceit that will serve as an excuse for eliminating them. *The people of Australia* is not so rank because it does not carry the suggestion that some mythic or historic force unites Australians in their destiny. But if we must have *as a people,* then *traditionally* has to go, and not only because *optimistically* is sitting on top of it. It has to go because it is so at odds with Australian history, it could be reasonably called a lie. *Traditionally* Australians built barriers against the world they are alleged to have engaged so *optimistically;* for one hundred years they built barriers against all nonwhite races and proclaimed a White Australia Policy; *traditionally* they clung to the mother country for protection against that same world; *traditionally* they took less an optimistic view of the world than an ironic, fatalistic view of the world. The smugness of the sentence about our being welcome guests and warm hosts is so larded with fantasy and self-delusion, it transcends *Neighbours* and becomes Dame Edna Everage.

The thought will occur at least to some Australian readers that it has been in their nature recently to play very cold hosts to uninvited guests. John Howard's warm hosts voted enthusiastically for a government that turned away refugees plucked from sinking boats in the Timor Sea, spread lies that these "people had thrown their children into the sea," and continues to hold men, women, and children in detention centers in the desert—or pays impoverished Pacific Island governments to incarcerate them on Australia's behalf.

These refugees are also called *queue jumpers, illegals,* and, on the assumption that they had thrown their children into the sea, *not the sort of people* Australians want coming into their country. With this bland rhetorical deceit the Australian government turned seeming defeat into a comfortable election victory. Fear and loathing do not require stridency or mass rallies; the most commonplace phrasing will do just as well to suspend reason and decency.

Given that recent history, we might wonder if the words are as ingenuous as they sound. The thought, even the subconscious thought, might have been of a piece with Medea's "soft talk." Thus—*as a people* Australians are very nice; people who don't agree with this proposition are not nice people; people who are not nice are not Australian in the sense of Australians *as a people*. People who are not prepared to be Australian *as a people* should shut up or piss off back to where they came from.

They're just words. And to say that they mean the opposite of what many people believe to be the facts is not to say that it's as rotten a thing as putting ARBEIT MACHT FREI (WORK LIBERATES) over the gates of Auschwitz. The Australian prime minister's language is platitudinous, unctuous, and deceitful. It is in bad taste. If it is not actual propaganda, it has much in common with it. Propaganda, as the Canadian philosopher John Ralston Saul says, is "the negation of language. It destroys memory and therefore removes any sense of reality." Abuse the language and you abuse the polity. If you construct a collective character and a mythic history and paint over them with invented virtues, you also abuse the people: you demean them and deny them their own history.

Myths are tempting to those who are in a position to

manipulate their fellow human beings, because a myth is sacred, and what is sacred cannot be questioned. That's where their power comes from. They simplify and provide meaning without the need of reason. Marketing and advertising like myths for this reason. They stifle doubt and provide relaxation and comfort. It is about here that they meet clichés, which are myths of language. "Men hide behind their clichés," as Ionesco said. But that is not a crime against humanity.

The Americans saying they *lost their innocence* on September 11, 2001, is a myth, and also a cliché. As Philip Roth said, the Al Qaeda attack produced an orgy of narcissism. Narcissism naturally spawns myths, myths of character and history, of *good* and *evil*. September 11 produced a torrent of American myths. The United States *innocent*? After slavery? After a Civil War? After the Puritans? After four hundred years, they're still *innocent*? It is like John Howard saying Australians *lost their innocence* when a lunatic ran riot and killed people at Port Arthur. Port Arthur—a notoriously vicious nineteenth-century British convict settlement—*innocent*? Australia *innocent*? It can only be fantasy, ignorance, or mischief—or a cliché that has lost its meaning through overuse and can be anything you want to make of it. It's one of those clichés that might as well be called a lie. It contradicts what is known and what ought to be known; it does not help us understand a tragedy but rather diminishes it. It insults our intelligence. We may as well claim descent from Teutonic knights as claim to be *innocent*. As public language, it is the equivalent of airbrushing.

The trite, the obscure, and the impenetrable readily become the deceitful. Instead of asking what the words mean, journalists tell us on behalf of the politician, as if the code is legitimate. At other times (it depends on the shape of the day's story) they take the most egregious nonsense at face value. Less frequently, but often enough to make you want to put a brick through the television or radio or cancel your subscription to the newspaper, they actually give points for evasive or incomprehensible language. They mean to say that the politician was clever enough to avoid the traps they set for him, but they may as well report: "the cabinet minister did very well at confounding his constituents today; really you have to admire the way he hides behind clichés and lies so sincerely."

Reporters who concentrated on the words would do more service to democracy. If only they would ask: "What do you mean by *innocence*?" "How many times can a country lose it?" "You're an American—were *you* innocent?" "Did you mean *ignorance*—Americans lost their *ignorance*?" And when they say *the American way*: "What *way* are you talking about there?" "Historically speaking?" "If it's the American tradition, as you say, which part of it?" "Open and expansive or parochial and paranoid?" "The tradition of violence or the hope of the world?"

These may be glib, facile questions, but when did that hold back a journalist? The difference between these questions and the usual glib, facile questions is that these oblige the powerful to enter regions where truth, though not assured, has a chance of revealing itself. It might complicate the task of spin doctors, sabotage clichés, and force our leaders into spontaneous thought and finding words for it.

Poll-driven politics demands that leaders stay *in touch* with the people, even if this means that they speak to us in the same tones and with the same clarity as the witnesses to

accidents and sport we see on television. The difference between the feigned spontaneity, outrage, and excitement
seen in authoritarian societies and dictatorships and that
seen in democratic leaders who are agitated only by what
agitates public opinion is a difference of degree. More commonly, our leaders are primed to insert the bit that is the
currency of political exchange—the grab or sound bite—regardless of the consequences for language, coherence, or
self-respect. This creates a curious and debilitating paradox:
to seem like ordinary people, our leaders try not to say anything too difficult or challenging. They feel they must say
something to maintain the impression that they *know* something. But they also feel compelled to say the thing that
will have the most effect, a pointed, distilled sort of thing
in what they reckon is language the mob will understand.

The result is that people of ordinary intelligence notice
something unnatural in their gestures and something distracted in their expression, because the politician can't hide
the fact that he's waiting for the chance to say what he's
been primed to say, and when he gets that chance he jumps
at it with unnatural haste. But because it's rehearsed it
doesn't sound natural, and chances are he will add some
dog-eared phrase like "at this particular point in time" or "a
window of opportunity" or "in terms of a window of opportunity" or "at the end of the day," and viewers will mentally
yawn as their brains struggle for oxygen and go back to the
ironing for stimulation. In his efforts to appear ordinary the
politician runs the risk that ordinary people will think him
inconsequential or a birdbrain, especially if he gets tangled
between the grab he's dredging from his memory and other
mental processes necessary to survive or think on your feet,
in which event he (in this case the U.S. president) might say

something like "You teach a child to read and he or her will be able to pass a literacy test"; or "More and more of our imports come from overseas"; or "I've been misunderestimated." Or, in reaching for something grand, he might say the family is where "our wings take dream."

It is sad that politicians rarely attempt to put their case complete with ambiguities and contradictions; that is to say, as ordinary people generally put their cases to each other. A politician of this kind might be very popular, especially if he also had beliefs and principles. But of course this is a difficult effect to achieve when you are talking through journalists, and your advisers' words are lying like dead things in a front chamber of your brain, or you have a script in front of you that you only half believe. It's out of daily political reportage that those dying phrases come spinning slowly, and, as they do with television soap operas, the people imitate them without meaning to. You'll hear them say *at this point in time* in workaday conversation, or *he would not resile* at funerals. I am grateful for this *window of opportunity* to pay tribute to my father. Or, *We will never forget the way Muriel pushed the envelope.* And then the people who write the soap operas hear it, and their characters begin to say they *will not resile* and they have *pushed the envelope;* and the language becomes less like a language and more like just what happens when you open your mouth, less like an expression of a mental process and more like gruel or reflux.

●

George Orwell was appalled by political language sixty years ago. He would be more appalled now. Friedrich Nietzsche, who a hundred years ago was appalled by nearly everything, would feel vindicated *and* appalled. So too

Flaubert, and many others after him who contemplated mass society with dread and loathing. "The entire dream of democracy is to raise the proletariat to the level of bourgeois stupidity," Flaubert wrote to George Sand soon after the horrors of the Paris Commune. That the bourgeoisie were stupid was clear from their pomposities and clichés. How much worse would it be when the peasants and workers started talking like that? "Masses, numbers, are invariably idiotic," he said. How to make universal suffrage and universal education the foundations of a country without creating universal folly? Flaubert believed it could not be done; but meanwhile, he said, the prospect of it would lead to terrible revolutions like the Commune, and the reality to terrible wars (like those of the twentieth century). George Sand had a more optimistic view: she said we must fix our hopes on the essential goodness of human nature (the French portion of it at least), and its capacity for love, bravery, and enlightenment.

Some of our contemporaries might say that Flaubert and Sand were both wrong and that it has proved a far better thing to fix our hopes on marketing, and, better still, to create a buyer's market. So this is the era of marketing, and so we speak its language: it might be crass, but it's an improvement on the era of world war and international revolution. The argument can't be lightly dismissed. Culture, language included, always has to pay a tithe to social progress and democracy. Standards are bound to slip. It's a perpetual and necessary trade-off to keep chaos and bloodshed at bay. Vulgarity is the price of freedom. Compromise is the price of having something left at the end.

But compromise is not capitulation: each party to a compromise has something the other side needs. You show them that there is a point beyond which you won't go and they can't without hurting themselves. That point, surely, has been reached with the language.

Orwell had his own problems with the rise of the working classes, equally despising the class system and the viciousness of mass movements to abolish it. In his famous 1946 essay "Politics and the English Language," and in *Animal Farm* and *1984,* he was principally concerned with the potential for language to function as a tool of totalitarian ideology. He saw this potential realized in the rhetoric of fascism and communism, in bureaucracy, in managerialism, and in pretentious and opinionated intellectuals. Wherever demagogues and bullies went, there also went obfuscation, pomposity, and doublespeak. For Orwell, the corruption of language in public life threatened the intelligent discourse on which democracy depends. Civilized society depends on the exercise of common sense, which depends upon our saying what we mean clearly enough for everyone of reasonable intelligence to understand. The political point follows from the general one Ben Jonson made: "Language springs out of the most retired and inmost parts of us, and is the image of the parent of it, the mind. No glass renders a man's form and likeness so true as his speech."

Democracy depends upon plain language. It depends upon common understanding. We need to feel safe in the assumption that words mean what they are commonly understood to mean. Deliberate ambiguities, slides of meaning, and obscure, incomprehensible, or meaningless words poison the democratic process by leaving people less able to make informed or rational decisions. They erode trust. Depleted language always comes with a depleted democracy: the language of undemocratic systems is proof enough of this. Where language is forced into unnatural shapes, the body politic is ugly.

We need not go as far as Orwell did: not all political language is designed to make lies sound truthful and murder respectable. Political language has this tendency, but Orwell sometimes turned tendencies into absolutes. Had Lincoln followed Orwell's rules for plain language, furthermore, the Gettysburg Address would have been a plain thing and only a fraction as effective; and Martin Luther King's "I Have a Dream" speech would have to be rendered without the dream. We cannot imagine Orwell talking about "words of interposition and nullification." As Primo Levi says, "Clarity is a necessary but not a sufficient condition: one can be clear and boring, clear and useless, clear and untruthful, clear and vulgar. . . ."

Public language benefits mightily from what a contemporary observed in the young Lincoln a decade before he became president: that he had "a curious vein of sentiment running through his thought, which is his most valuable mental attribute." Contemporary Orwellians also need to be reminded that abolishing clichés, doublespeak, and buzzwords will not in itself make truth and justice flourish. But to aim toward this happy state (even to *benchmark* it) is sensible because it might do good, as much good as, for instance, reforming the Upper House of Parliament or abolishing the House of Lords, and with less chance of unanticipated strife.

Corrupted language is an indispensable source of humor. Groucho and Chico Marx got half their jokes from corrupted language. It is one of comedy's oldest routines to stretch the language to the point of breaking, or mimic those who do it naturally. But no comic could do much better than George W. Bush, the man who has some claim to be the most powerful the world has ever known, when he says, just like Chico: "He can't take the high horse and then claim the low road"; or throttles his Savior's message into ersatz narcissism, "We must all hear the universal call to like your neighbor just like you like to be liked yourself." Chico might have said that too.

All totalitarian regimes, regardless of their ideological origin, pervert language to delude, intimidate, and mystify their subjects. They also take the humor out of it, even when the circumstances are laughable. Stalin sent his erstwhile comrades to their deaths confessing ludicrously concocted crimes, and countless intelligent people were persuaded to believe them. What is it that torture and brainwashing try to extract? Words. They need the word as well as the corpse. If words define reality, you cannot control the one without controlling the other. This helps explain Stalin's obsession with writers (and musicians), and perhaps also occasional outbursts against them in open societies where casual indifference is the norm. In the so-called culture wars of recent years, an effort has been made to ignore them pointedly. Politicians regularly discover words to label amorphous categories of malcontents as irrelevant or stupid. *Elite, chattering classes, urban intellectuals, academic,* and countless others are, like *peasant* and *provincial,* insipid in their usual environment; but, like certain animals and chemical compounds, they become poisonous and destructive in a political one.

There is an old vein of anti-intellectualism in this, and another one of making scapegoats. And a third insists that artists, like their distant cousins in universities, accept managerial classifications. Writers and painters now work in an arts *industry,* where they can be expected to do what people do in other industries, namely, *add value, continuously improve,* and become *world class.* These managerial terms reveal a managerial *ideology* at work, a set of ideas refined into a self-reinforcing belief system.

In this case, weirdly, the ideology managerialism most resembles is a debased Marxism. Isolating artists and intellectuals, or offering them a choice between frightening, often fatal isolation and fatally compromised incorporation, is an old and sinister theme of history. Not that the language of management leads by even circuitous roads to the Gulag; but neither does it open the way to all the virtues of an open society. Similarly, dubbing everyone whose reading of history leads them to conclusions different from the preferred ones *black-armband historians;* channeling frustrations felt by the politically powerless to the *politically correct;* isolating *chattering classes* and *elites* from a pretended mainstream—all these and many terms of political abuse are common and inevitable in democracies—and all have parallels in tyrannies.

We need not believe Norman Mailer when he insists that the United States is proto-fascist, but it is wise just the same to keep an eye on politicians for signs that they are traducing not just opposing politicians but constituents whose thinking doesn't suit them. Watch how, in lieu of actual exile, dissenters are labeled *illegitimate.* When the words are suspicious, go after them, insist they tell us what they mean. Go after the *meaning* of the words. And if the speakers say they are the kind who call things as they see them, that they don't mince words, and *call a spade a spade,* go after them even harder. They're often the worst liars of the lot.

We citizens have intuition, natural skepticism, and powers of analysis to go on, but we still rely on facts and in the end have to trust our leaders to tell us what is actually the case. Whether it's a lie, a half-truth, a weasel word, a banality, a buzzword, or a cliché, if we are misled by it our rights are reduced in proportion. Words are bullets. They are also good for smothering, strangling, and poisoning, and for hiding murderous intentions from your victims (and sometimes from yourself). The Nazis called their plans to exterminate millions of people by industrial means *the Final Solution,* which was no less a lie than informing families of concentration camp inmates that their son or brother or father or mother had died *while attempting to escape.* Every war throws up new corruptions (*wastage* from World War I, *collateral damage* from World War II, *deconfliction, attrited,* and *degraded* from Iraq) and at the same time, as Hemingway said, they make old words like *honor* and *glory* sound obscene.

George W. Bush's words are generally less menacing and more laughable, but they live in the same murky region where language is broken and remolded into bizarre shapes to satisfy the needs of power. So we should be concerned when the world's most powerful man makes speeches of this kind.

I know America wants reconciliation and unity. I know Americans want progress. And we must seize this moment and deliver. Together, guided by a spirit of common sense, common courtesy and common goals, we can unite and inspire the American citizens. . . . Together we will make all our public schools excellent, teaching every student of every background and every accent, so that no child is left behind. . . . Together we will address some of society's deepest problems one person at a time, by encouraging the good hearts and good works of the American people. . . . I have faith that with God's help we as a nation will move forward as one nation, indivisible.

But if God can read between the lines, he's not going to fall for what an earlier generation of American commentators might have called *bomfog* or *flapdoodle* or *tomfoolery* or *hokum* or so much *hornswaggle*. *"All our schools excellent"?* *"Every student"?* *"One person at a time"?* With the greatest respect, we don't think so. Not even with *common courtesy* behind us. It's not just the disingenuousness, the outrageous promises that insult our common sense; it's the tired prose, the dead words: *encouraging, empowering, reconciliation, unity, together, no child is left behind. Together we will address* . . . Perhaps that's what they do in Texas. *Yeehah! Let's go addressing!*

These lists have all the moral force of the copy on a cereal packet, and in much the same way combine the ultramundane ("These oatflakes contain carbohydrates. . . ." What oats don't?) and the outrageous (". . . to get you through the day." You mean we won't make it without them?) Add niacin, riboflavin, and vitamins A, B, and C and you'll get through your day just like the magnificent athlete in the picture on the packet gets through his. *Together* is the carbohydrate of this speech; *common courtesy, common sense,* etc., are, if you like, the vitamins and minerals. The cereal advertising turns a need (nutrition) into a want (health and beauty), for which read hopeless desire. The political speech works on the same formula. The breakfast table and the podium: marketing triumphs at both venues. And not only in Texas. The speech might as well have been written in London, Canberra, or Wellington, Liberal or Conservative. Vapidity is an *international* political language.

U.S. presidents are more than ciphers; but watching them, you wonder if the essential purpose of their existence is to read speeches that are, in the main, confections of American myths and ideals. Sometimes they are in Frontierland, sometimes Tomorrowland. A president is at different times a cowboy, a sheriff, a general, a statesman, a down-home all-American boy: John Wayne, Teddy Roosevelt, George Patton, Huck Finn; log cabin to White House; Harvard Business School to White House. Remember the Alamo! Remember the Twin Towers! The prose can be grandiloquent, but it is always predictable.

> We will not tire, we will not falter, and we will not fail. . . . I will not yield; I will not rest; I will not relent in any way in this struggle for freedom and security for the American people.

A presidential speech has this much in common with country and western music—we know what chord is coming next and what words: "alone" will follow "phone," "you" will follow "do" or "true," "heart," "apart," and so on until you feel you've been baptized in warm treacle. Yet, because the president is reading complete and shapely sentences, his performance is invested with a sort of old-world grace, a period quality that in a kitsch culture suggests the authentic past, even the eternal. And the ghosts of the dead it brings forth, and all those American dreams and everything that made the country great, and everything the enemies of freedom want to destroy, combine irresistibly with the flag draped behind him, and millions of viewers find that their hands have crept over hearts that are beating that much stronger.

Public language has its origins in power, in the executive decrees of priests, rulers, and their subalterns. It is the language of the mighty—or the meretricious—mediated for us by democratic sentiment or the perceived need to take account of it. Thus, when George W. Bush delivers his State of the Union address to Congress, he veers strategically between the unfettered belligerence of a real emperor whose might is unquestionable and the sanctimony of a phony one whose might derives in some measure from the people. He says *We will prevail,* not *I will prevail,* and if the effect is to make many viewers suspect that by *we* he means himself, Dick Cheney, Donald Rumsfeld, and a handful of unseen others, it's still held to be better than the egotistical *I*.

Balancing your ego with your constituents' egos is one of the essential arts of leadership, and because language is the main mediator in this, it is a daily concern for speechwriters. Here is Hillary Clinton adjusting the balance in the modern democratic way.

> I think that in everyday ways, how you treat your disappointments, and whether you forgive the pain that others cause you, and frankly, to acknowledge the pain you cause to others, is one of the biggest challenges we face as we move into the next century.

Frankly, another big challenge as we move into the next century is avoiding cliché. I think, speaking of *everyday ways,* we could begin by not saying *challenge.* It only *seems* necessary.

We need not argue with Hillary Clinton's sentiments. Countless magazines and daytime television are expressly created for the moments when you feel you must go public with them. But if she (along with much of the English-speaking world) were not so habituated to the word "challenge," she might have taken her idea to some less bizarre conclusion and left us less worried about a world run by American Democrats. Without "challenge" playing fridge to her magnet, she might have said only that we will be happier when we learn to cope with pain and disappointment. This at least gets it in proportion, even if it is not much different from saying we will be happier when we are happier. But that's where solipsism takes you, and it's an important part of the economy these days. Without the cant word "challenge" drawing her on, she might not have felt compelled to rank coping with unhappiness among the *biggest challenges we face as we move into the next century,* along with other *challenges* like Africa, the Middle East, and nuclear weapons, we presume. And she might have thought just long enough to remember that old Job was coping with pain and disappointment well before daytime television got hold of it.

Orwell might groan, but Nietzsche would yawn. Nietzsche had less faith in people of reasonable intelligence: democracy was a political system calculated to make the intelligent minority subject to the will of the stupid. Of course, then, the language of democracy is impoverished and corrupted—or moronic, to use a favorite word of Nietzsche's most famous American disciple, H. L. Mencken. Moronic like the morons democracy puts in charge.

Nietzsche would very likely say the language of democracy merely reflects the *nature* of democracy; the corruptions of language are not aberrations any more than electing mediocrities to high office is an aberration. When George W. Bush speaks, we're getting the real thing. It is the mass we are hearing—or, more precisely, language that has been programmed for their level of intelligence and interest. When the Texan unfurls his vision in chaotic or strategized prose, it is just as Nietzsche (and Flaubert and all the others) said it would be.

The question is not easily settled, but the trend toward a globalized culture dominated by a great mass democracy of unprecedented power in the world (including the power to infantilize it) might favor the Nietzschean view over Orwell's. So might regional imitations of American-style poll-driven politics, the triumph of free market economics, managerialism, and other species of philistine self-interest, including the universal narcissism that is an inevitable by-product of a market-driven society and necessary to keep it running.

If Nietzsche is right, attempts to arrest the decline of language are equivalent to arresting history, which is to say a waste of time—one such, indeed, as only a moron could conceive. We can give up the wait for an inspiring word from our leaders and look forward to everyone talking like a *knowledge manager.*

Knowledge managers talk like this: *frameworks . . . based upon reflection in action, pragmatic real world systems implementations, as well as theory and practice defining research conducted over the past two decades.* They talk like this because *knowledge management*

> caters to the critical issues of organizational adaption, survival, and competence in face of increasingly discontinuous environmental changes. . . . Essentially it embodies organizational processes that seek synergistic combination of data and information processing capacity

of information technologies and the creative and innovative capacity of human beings.

Let's defer to the *bottom line*: let's try to quantify it. What costs the culture more, the theft of a Matisse or a rare manuscript, or rafts of consultants telling the institutions in which they are housed that they need *structural envisioning*? To *envision structurally* is to

- Build structural options by activity/process, output, and customer
- Select a model to explore/develop process/output combination
- Refine structural concept, develop notional function hooks for key processes and outputs

(Later they intend *to test the structural concept by assigning the accountabilities to* [the] *notional functional hooks,* but doubtless that is another story, and probably will be billed separately.) The Matisse and the manuscript at least had worth while they existed; they were seen, remembered, copied. But what is the worth of *structural envisioning*? And what has it to do with conserving and displaying manuscripts and paintings?

Far from being sued or jailed for this, the consultants ask for and invariably receive very large amounts of money for *their efforts*. Politicians who confound us in the same way—who say, for instance, that they are *committed* to a library or a gallery when for all that means they may as well face in its direction and blow their noses—also go free; many of them indeed with an airline Gold Pass and abundant superannuation. Doubtless the business, bureaucratic, and political classes would all be inclined to defend themselves by pointing to the success of the national economy, or its corporate equivalent, the *bottom line*. Up against the wall, were we ever able to get them there, they might even try the one about their own success being proof against the allegations. Why would they pay me this much if I wasn't doing something right? A professional wrestler would say the same. The well rewarded have *always* said it. Press them hard and they will tell you that the present *scenario,* including the BMW, is the work of God.

•

The art of connecting words creates shades of meaning. This makes it an art of deep importance, because a shade of meaning is as consequential as a fundamental difference. I don't need to be utterly wrong; being slightly wrong will mislead just as well. If I say *"Ms. Kidman is little short of sensational in the role,"* it means one thing; but by adding nothing more than an "a," to make *"Ms. Kidman is a little short of sensational in the role,"* I make my meaning suddenly more obscure, ambiguous, possibly ironic, mischievous, or even contemptuous. If I say *axis of evil* when, for all the proofs of *evil* there is no evidence of an *axis* existing, I am as likely to cause as much confusion as if I had said *axle of evil* or *praxis of evil* or something even more ridiculous. If I say *nests of evil,* or *governments with evil in common,* the confusion will likely take a different form and, because it is a more accurate description, it is likely there will be less of it. It is not the context but the words that shape the meaning here. Each word is a weapon of a different kind and wounds in different ways.

Meaning is also determined by who says the words and how. It helps if it is someone with a claim to wisdom, for example. But then, someone who is wise might not choose what, by any definition, is the wrong word—"axis." Someone concerned about shades of meaning—and concerned about the consequences of getting them wrong—might not choose evil." "Evil" is a word without shades, which means the accuser best be without sin. And since the word is absolute, there is risk in using it selectively. It might seem to sanction "evil" beyond the *axis,* while those within it conclude they're being picked on and wonder if *the words* have less to do with *evil* than with certain strategic ambitions. A wise person, or a cautious or disinterested person, might not say *axis of evil;* but a cunning person might.

A cunning person might say "evil" as often as is necessary to make himself feel good, or his constituents feel both good about themselves and fond of him for making them feel that way. For the same kind of reasons the word "illegals" is attractive to people who do not want refugees or asylum seekers in their country. In Australia "queue jumpers" worked the same way. The people seeking asylum had broken no Australian law, and there had been no queue for them to jump. But the terms were not intended to describe reality, but rather to twist and conceal it in a way that would incite contempt and fear. Words like these, as Norman Mailer says, get to be addictive: you press the button once and it seems to work, so you press it again and again. That's why in a democracy it pays to listen carefully: don't read their lips, read their words.

To be *useful* in political language is not the same thing as being clear. In fact, it's very often the opposite. "Compassionate conservatism" (a relative term if ever there was one) proved useful to the president of the United States and the Republican Party, but it has been four years since

George W. Bush first used it and still no one knows what it means. By the time this book is published, quite possibly no one will be using "moral clarity." Socrates, St. Augustine, and Kant, among others who fretted all their lives about the subject, may rest easier in their graves. *Moral clarity* is not so much an idea as a buzzword: a *you're in/you're out* word, as "liberal" is in modern America and "liberalistic" was in Hitler's Germany. It is an intellectual way of saying, "Just do it!" and watching to see who jumps. The enemies of *moral clarity* are waverers and bleeding hearts who are, the argument goes, *moral relativists*. Moral relativists are, if not friends of terrorists and rogues, less patriotic and American than Americans possessed of *moral clarity*. *Moral relativists* are closely related to *cultural relativists,* and it is *cultural relativists,* of course, who tie the country in knots pleading multiculturalism and the case for the rights of non–English speakers. This is not to say that it is patriotic to despise all forms of relativism: if you did that, you might be less inclined to favor *low-yield* nuclear weapons, which are relative, surely, to where you're standing when they go off. It is impossible to be an imperial power—or even a politician (God-fearing or not)—without exercising some degree of *moral relativism*. It's very difficult to fight a war without exercising it, and quite impossible to market one. The problem is apparent in terms like *humane war, surgical strike,* and *smart bomb:* they are *relatively* humane, surgical, and smart. *Weapons of Mass Destruction* is another relative term (though perhaps less relative than President Bush's "weapons of mass destruction–related activities"). Some WMD are much more destructive than others, and some not called WMD are plainly capable of causing mass destruction. Some, as the British politician Robin Cook has tried to explain, sound like

WMD—a vial of anthrax, for instance—but are not. And then there are WMD that don't exist: WMD that the proponents of *moral clarity* have invented for their own purposes. Thus "moral relativism" is put at the service of "moral clarity." Nevertheless, "moral clarity" is an extraordinarily useful term, and it is a wonder someone did not think of it earlier, especially someone living in a country founded by Puritans.

In April 2003 we heard less of "moral clarity" but "vital role" was everywhere. We heard of the *vital role* of the United Nations in Iraq. The *vital role* of Australia, Spain, and Britain in Iraq. The *vital role* of the Iraqis in Iraq. No one, however, seemed to know what it meant, or if they did, they weren't saying. Thus our leaders insist on *moral clarity* but not verbal clarity. It is puzzling that the same people can be confident about a subject on which some of history's greatest minds cannot agree, yet confounded by the meaning of a simple phrase of their own making.

We need not waste time puzzling about it. In modern media-driven politics, words are chosen less for their meaning than for their ability to do the job. In business and politics words are not so much uttered as *implemented*. With *moral clarity* they *implement* a mace: with *vital role* a shield or smoke screen. Pursue them further (as if anybody does!) and they will *implement* a red herring, a snow job, a complete stonewall, or the next question.

When her long career was over, the soprano Magda Olivero said that the notes she sang divinely were not just notes but "expressions of the soul." Each time she went onstage, she said, "A halo opened . . . a magic halo. I would enter this magic halo and only leave it at the end of the opera." When the president of the United States stands before the U.S. Congress to deliver the State of the Union, one might expect him to experience something similar. He doesn't have the music, but the moment is his for commanding: a magnificent stage, a captive audience, the most sophisticated audio equipment and teleprompters, a script that has been honed and rehearsed for weeks. It is a moment of pure power. It is the rhetorical moment, the moment when traditionally the politician becomes the artist, reaching into his own deep sensibilities to inspirit or enlighten the thoughts and feelings of his audience. Or share them. Or confirm them. This rhetoric is also called leadership. It is—or was—the means by which leaders create a public frame of reference for events. To lead successfully is to have the people perceive things through that frame. Today the frame is called the *story* or the *message*.

But watching presidents in this most operatic of political settings, hardly ever are we moved—not, at least, we sympathetic observers at the outer reaches of his influence. It's the lack of music, of course, and even if they could perform the dramatic equivalent of Callas in *Tosca,* we are raised to be suspicious if not downright hostile to politicians who use operatic techniques. We've seen the images of Hitler, and if one of our own tries that sort of thing, we want him tied up and carted away at once. In the end it may be that the words are overwhelmed by the performing moment. We can hear a singer—any kind of singer—sing a song a hundred times, and if it's a good song, or it has some significance in our lives, it will move us. Perhaps it's the "vein of sentiment" in them. But when we watch a political leader perform today, the words come in a supporting role to all the other forces enlisted to serve the message.

The media conspire in this by asking if he looked the

part, if his timing was good, and if he sounded confident. They also ask if the politics were smart; will it play well in the marginals—*was he hunting where the ducks are,* as some Americans say. Had Lincoln been asked those questions after Gettysburg, his speech might easily have been called a failure. Policy—what the president says he'll *do*—is also an important measure but only one of several. The language of the speech is separated from the idea, which may be why it seems like ventriloquism and why these days it is customary to think of rhetoric as "empty"—not as argument but as gloss or trickery.

Long on rhetoric, short on substance, our commentators will say of a "Gettysburg-style" address—as they would have said about Lincoln's original. *A grab bag of promises,* they might say of a policy speech, and declare that the politician had failed to inspire or effectively pitch his program. And if he does attempt this, they will say it was a *blatant* pitch to some part of the populace, a pitch so *transparent,* in fact, that no voter is ever going to fall for it. Next time our politician tries to score on all fronts, and only adds to the record yet another rhetorical henhouse. The lesson is: words cut off from the impulse that created them are often as good as dead. They are so far from being "expressions of the soul," the greatest prima donna could not save them.

Much as we would like to hear them, we need something more from politics than "expressions of the soul." Politics is an argument; it should engage the intellect as well as the emotions. When only the emotions (or the prejudices, or the fantasies, or myths and ideology) are engaged, we smell deceit. We think the chances are we're being fooled or shortchanged; and if we don't think it, chances are we have been. The words our leaders use are the base material of an honest polity and a good society. Language is fundamental to democracy because, once we've done with the show business and analyzed the facial tics and gestures, the words are all we have to go on.

That is why we should not vote for any politician who says, for instance, *there are no quick fixes* more than three times a year. Punish her for banality and the contempt for us that it implies.

Attack the words and we might get closer to what we need from them: evidence of a mind, ideas, arguments, signs of conscientious effort and disinterested reasoning, a hint of imagination. We want to see what they are offering us and what they offer the country. By this we mean the opposite of platitudes, the sausage meat of politics: we mean what they are offering us in the way of leadership, management, government. If they can turn loaves into haddocks, good, but we will be satisfied to see some evidence that they understand their duties and our lives. We like to see a sign that they know what irritates us, what we hope for, and what makes us despair. We want to know if they *get it*. That does not mean we only want to hear calculated echoes of what we, the public, think; we would also be grateful for something to think about. There is idealism in this, but democracy is an ideal, and it needs idealism. And critics of ideals. It needs the arguments. This makes the public language fundamental.

There is an argument that as the public realm declines, so too must the public language. An empty public realm means a proportionately empty public language. People living in affluent, free market economies have no need or desire for visionary or charismatic leaders, or for the ennobling, inspiring, binding rhetoric with which they build their influence. Who needs a narcissist to lead a narcissistic society?

Who will respect power when everyone's *empowered*? When there is a remote control in every room with a television, and a host of channels, which ambitious leader is going to pass up style for substance, a cliché for a complex sentence, an image for an argument?

Politicians are now so conscious of the boundaries of safety and opportunity, they speak as if what they are describing has been decided in advance of them, as indeed it has, by polls and focus groups. They say what the people want to hear, and not what they will do. If to be human is to believe passionately, to be willful, funny, and powerful, they make a great effort not to be human. At the extreme end of this moderation, politics appears to have collided with what the postmodern calls "the death of the author." There are democratic states governed by people of such little apparent personality or belief, they seem to exist only to fulfill the basic requirement of democracy that the media and the people have someone to judge. We no longer see or hear politicians whose words spring directly from conviction, or in whom power obviously lives. These things, the realities of politics, are kept out of sight. Writing, Victor Serge said, should be "a testimony to the vast flow of life through us." Serge was a revolutionary, but his belief fits well enough with all democratic sentiment. When did you last hear "testimony to the vast flow of life" in the public language?

While the polls distill the popular position to bloodless caution, it is possible that the people could stand a little more excitement. It seems incredible that since September 11, 2001, no leader has uttered words that will ring forever in our minds, or even for a year or two. True, there's no Lincoln among them, or a Kennedy, a Roosevelt, or even a Clinton. But our leaders might look elsewhere for inspiration their imagination can't provide. They might look in the language. We should never miss an opportunity to quote things by others, as Proust said; they are "always more interesting than those one thinks up oneself." But there has not been so much as a "Farewell, sweet prince . . ." or "Why should a horse, a dog, a rat have breath . . ." Not these days: our leaders think up nothing and look up nothing.

And yet people like good words. Play them Martin Luther King and they will listen and you can be sure in any audience of a dozen one or two will brush away tears. This is at least partly because King understood how like a song a speech can be. But then, someone reading them the Gettysburg Address, or George Washington's speech when he stepped down from the presidency, or Roosevelt's on becoming president in the middle of the Depression will also move people, because the language and the thoughts are powerful.

Here is Roosevelt's sinewy inauguration address in 1933, very different in style from President Bush's 2001 address to Congress, and bearing a very different message about fear.

> This is pre-eminently the time to speak the truth, the whole truth, frankly and boldly. Nor need we shrink from honestly facing conditions in our country today . . . So first of all let me assert my firm belief that the only thing we have to fear is fear itself—nameless, unreasoning, unjustified terror which paralyzes needed efforts to convert retreat into advance.

It is not particularly original prose, but all the words are strung on the same taut thread: when he wants to emphasize a thought, like the thought about "fear itself," he tightens the thread, and it resonates like a guitar string. You can't avoid the meaning and once you've heard it, you remember it.

Words *can* be like notes, like expressions of the soul. They can make our hair stand up, they can lift our understanding to a higher plane, make us see things differently. They can inspire love and hope. You can see it happen before your eyes. Words can create a magic halo. But they have to have some thought or sentiment attached, and, like notes, be skillfully arranged.

When people make speeches, they attempt an embrace. They say to their audience, "you and me both": we are for all practical purposes the same. Martin Luther King did it in sentences that swept his audience across the United States—"from the prodigious hilltops of New Hampshire . . . to the curvaceous slopes of California," and many places in between. FDR did it, comparing the troubles of Americans in 1933 with "the perils which our forefathers conquered." Pericles, Lincoln, and Mark Antony all did it in their own way. It's a universal device: it says we are all one, with one profound inheritance, and one ideal to live up to. Speech-making is an exercise in welding people together by welding them to whatever it is they have in common, be it their landscape, their ancestors, their ambitions, even their language.

Politicians rarely get to make speeches as far-reaching as Martin Luther King at the Lincoln Memorial; but they can say similar things when they open a preschool in an outer suburb or a medical center in a country town. They can talk about the suburban frontier. They can set a new housing estate against the nation's history and the nation's values.

They can do the same in the country town, except here they will talk about what it is that people have never ceased to value in rural life. And not for nothing our politician will be seen soon afterward patting cows and dogs and babies—because if he got his words right, that is what he has just done with the people. He has stroked them, comforted them, bonded with them—told them that far from being forgotten, they are a priceless asset, part of the heroic national story and frequently on his mind.

Satire, Jonathan Swift said, is a kind of glass wherein the beholder sees everyone but himself. A political leader—the very opposite of a satirist—constructs a speech as the very opposite kind of mirror, one wherein, he hopes, every beholder will see himself. The idea has something in common with Proust's observation that "In reading every reader is, while he is reading, the reader of his own self." Every listener to a political speech is asking: Does he know who I am? What I think? What I need? What I am entitled to? This is the politician's bait: if he has a feel for them he can strew it on the water, watch them rise, and catch them with his idea. But it takes more than a photograph with the local manager or the football team. It amounts to more than just being seen there. Some imaginative effort is required, some knowledge of the local landscape and some understanding of history, some ideas and character. It requires a bit of psychological insight.

To be more than an exercise in spin, a mere gesture, or a confection for the media, democratic politics needs the language. It is one thing to have us eating from the palms of their hands, another to nourish us.

•

CONCLUSION

•

" . . . and yet his words, like cavalry horses answering the bugle, group themselves automatically into the familiar dreary pattern. This invasion of one's mind by ready-made phrases (lay the foundations, achieve a radical transformation) can only be prevented if one is constantly on guard against them, and every such phrase anaesthetizes a portion of one's brain."
    —GEORGE ORWELL, "POLITICS AND THE ENGLISH LANGUAGE"

•

"They risk-taked all night."
    —FOOTBALL COMMENTATOR

•

"This has been tough weeks in that country."
    —GEORGE W. BUSH

•

"Demonstrate and articulate innovative methodologies that will enhance your ability to have your ideas heard (influence) and actioned (project managed)."
    —UNIVERSITY LEADERSHIP AND PROFESSIONAL DEVELOPMENT PROGRAM

•

"The group brings together key people across the Office of Education, the Office of Learning and Teaching, and the Office of Strategy and Resources. . . . The group meets regularly to ensure we develop a shared understanding of the core initiatives and to discuss key issues that emerge. By addressing the interdependencies of the initiatives, within the overarching framework of the Blueprint, the group is able to support a cohesive communication strategy to principals and schools. In addition, each construct requires the central office staff to

engage deeply with the concepts that underpin each of the initiatives. A range of processes has been used to explore issues and gather feedback from different stakeholders to inform our thinking."
—EDUCATION DEPARTMENT, VICTORIA, AUSTRALIA

•

"I write as well as I can on each occasion."
—ITALO CALVINO

•

THE CASE MADE IN THIS BOOK DOES NOT LEND ITSELF TO barricades and rallies. It does not reduce to slogans, and if it did, who would shout them? People will march to save a cultural institution, some threatened corner of a way of life, or a clump of trees, but they will not rally for the language. Not physically at least.

I have written this essay in the hope that awareness might increase in some small degree and with it indignation—a small degree and a not very sanguine hope because I know that powerful forces, including possibly the whole tide of history, are against us. "Does literature, does reading, does literary analysis, change anything except consciousness?" the critic Don Anderson asked a few years ago, and answered his own question: sadly, with rare exceptions, no.

Substitute "works of the imagination" for "poetry," he said, and Auden has it about it right.

For poetry makes nothing happen: it survives
In the valley of its making where executives
Would never want to tamper . . .

The same is true if we substitute a plea for "imaginative language," or "language from which the imagination is not excluded," or just "real language." Real language makes "nothing happen": not by itself, not when lousy language will do as well.

Still, it is not a small thing to change consciousness, and so long as we are powerless to change experience, we'll settle for it. The greater part of the struggle over language will have to be conducted with language. How else did managerialism impose itself on all our lives if not with words? With marketing, no doubt, and PowerPoint, the profit motive, huge natural advantages, and all kinds of tricks, including fear. But with words they conveyed the creed that exiles us, and words are the only means of fighting back.

The principal tactic is counterassertion: they say, *deconfliction,* we say *Claptrap! Hogwash!* And we say it *every* time—mockingly, aggressively, in sorrow, in anger. We can also turn our backs every time they say it, drape our handkerchiefs on our heads, or tap our pens furiously. We can try being a refusenik and say we will not answer such a letter, much less send a check. And mock them, never stop mocking them.

People seeking a more creative solution might propose in their workplaces a twelve-month moratorium on selected words and phrases. This will improve the public language, first, by ridding it of some dull and stupid pests; second, by obliging writers, speakers, and researchers to rediscover good words that have fallen into disuse; and third, by encouraging those responsible for what the rest of us have to read and hear to respect our most precious cultural inheritance. This is a limited preliminary list, and the effects will not be immediate. But as more people become conscious of the *issue*, they will stop saying "issue" and search for fresher and more precise words. "Problem" will not do. Reference books will find a way into their lives. They will have conversations about language with their colleagues and friends. Without "issue" to fall back on, they will come up with words like "disease," "plague," "myxomatosis," "sclerosis," "edema," "predicament," and "dilemma." 'Paradox" will be rediscovered.

Organizations can set monthly, quarterly, and yearly targets for expunging words and discovering them. Inevitably, language consultancies will sprout in every town and city, but they will have to go by a different name, because if ever a word needed abolishing, it is "consultant."

Overall, the effect should one day stand comparison with the desert around Ayers Rock when cattle and other hard-hoofed animals were fenced out: it bloomed into a natural garden of infinite variety. When you see it, the wonder is to think this splendor had been there all along, buried, waiting. As language is. Those with no feeling for the natural world might find more inspiration in the example of the free market once liberated from the slovenly and oppressive interventions of governments. The lesson is the same however you learn it: these words clog the language and cut us off from thought, feeling, and possibility.

Here are some words to set the ball rolling, and some synonyms that also serve as a very modest sample of words that could be substituted for the proscribed ones. A useful exercise is attached to each entry.

•

GLOSSARY

Action/actioned/actioning: (*v.*) Do, act, act upon, carry out, implement, etc. (As in "Who will *action* the implementation process?" or "Geoffrey will be responsible for the implementation of the *actioning* of it." To put into play or effect. "*Actioning* what comes naturally." To organize a meeting; prepare a document; hire a consultant, auditor, or plumber; open a door; get the coffee, etc. "Don't just stand there. *Action* something!" (Note: "What is *actioned* cannot be un*actioned*.")

EXERCISE: What is Macbeth on about here?
"If it were actioned when 'tis actioned, then 'twere well it were actioned quickly."

Bottom line: Line at the bottom, nethermost, as far down as one can go, etc. Gross sales less taxes, interest, depreciation, etc. Net earnings. Net income. Net profit. Net.

The balance. (As in "All managers must keep an eye on the *bottom line*.") What it comes down to. That to which everything reduces or must be reduced. The minimum acceptable. (As in "What's your *bottom line*?") What's left when the bullshit is stripped away. The nub, gist, meaning, core meaning, kernel, core kernel, core, key, substance, sum, content, import, true measure, significance, essence, pith, meat, burden, the heart of it, etc. (As in "Do you love me? That's the *bottom line*, Brian.")

EXERCISE: What's the *bottom line* here? Does Hamlet know? "Not a whit, we defy augury: there is a special providence in the fall of a sparrow. If it be now, 'tis not to come; if it be not to come, it will be now; if it be not now, yet it will come—the readiness is all. Since no man owes of aught he leaves, what is't to leave betimes?"

Closure: The act of closing or shutting. The act of enclosing or that which encloses. Bringing to a conclusion. Something satisfactorily completed, e.g., a business deal (as in "Do you want to revisit the critical deliverables or do we have *closure*?"); a relationship (as in "So long as she's got the teak sideboard, I can't have *closure*"); an argument or other dramatic episode; a life (as in "Harry had *closure* yesterday, after a long illness"). A favorable outcome, especially in law, including the award of a substantial amount of money, a long prison sentence, or the death penalty for one's opponent. *Closure* is often indicated where grief, depression, frustration, loathing, and envy are present. One's enemies—and they are numerous—try to prevent us from achieving *closure*. What one tries to achieve; what life's about, etc.

EXERCISE: Was Hamlet wishing for *closure*?
   "To die, to sleep—no more; and by a sleep to say we end the heartache and the thousand natural shocks that flesh is heir to.'Tis a consummation devoutly to be wish'd."

Commit/committed/commitment: An expression of resolve, intent, loyalty, fealty, fidelity, willingness, faith, dedication, devotion, determination, etc. An interest or belief in another person, an animal such as a dog or racehorse, a thing, a policy, a club or employer or oneself, etc. An attachment to someone, something, or oneself. A pledge or oath (As in "With this ring I thee *commit* myself to.") Duty. Passion. Obsession. (As in "I have an absolute *commitment* to you, darling.") An intention to do something. (As in "I am *committed* to going to the ends of the earth with you, my precious.")

EXERCISE: Rewrite the following sentence without "committed:"
   "At the end of the day, in terms of his other interests, Edward was not *committed* enough to the throne."

Core: (cf. **key**) The center, heart, or truth of something, the bit you throw away, not. (As in "*core* policy," "*core* commitment," "*core* strategy," etc.) The hard, pithy, or stringy bit. The essential thing about it. Also **non-core** (as in "That was a *non-core* promise.")

EXERCISE: Rewrite the following sentence without "core" (or "key"):

> "The commitment I made not to introduce a goods and service tax was not a *core* promise. It was a *non-core* promise."

Customer: One who purchases goods or services—*any* goods or services. A client. An airline passenger. A recipient of secret intelligence. A person in receipt of social welfare payments and other assistance. An inmate of a mental asylum or prison. A patient in a hospital. A resident of a nursing home. A taxpayer (as in "The Taxation Office employs around twenty thousand people across the country and manages in excess of eleven million *customers*. . . .") A citizen. A person, including a child. Any organization or section of an organization, including a section of the same organization that receives something from another organization or section. Companies and other organizations describe themselves as *customer-focused* or *customer-centric* and speak of *enhanced customer experiences*.

EXERCISE: Improve on these lyrics:

> "*Customers, customers* who need *customers,*
> Are the luckiest *customers* in the world."

Deliver/deliverable: Release from bondage; assist in child-birth; pass to intended recipient; fulfill a promise. Do whatever you said you would do (as in "We will *deliver* on child care," "We have *delivered* on jobs," "We have *delivered* on reform"). Companies *deliver* on service, efficiency, productivity, the bottom line, etc. They *deliver* to "all our stakeholders." Footballers, athletes, racehorses, etc., *deliver*—or if they squander their talent, they fail to *deliver*. Consultants *deliver* training packages, knowledge management skills, etc. ('. . . her experience with direct investments enables her to *deliver* insight into this area"). The most common thing to be *delivered* is an *outcome*. A possible or desirable outcome is a *deliverable;* a highly desirable outcome is a *key deliverable*. *Deliver* us from evil—is a key *deliverable* if it can be done.

EXERCISE: Try singing this:
"And more, much more than this,
I *delivered* it my way."

Empower/empowered/empowerment: To give power, including *self-empowerment* (*n.*), *empowering* (*adj.*), strengthen, vivify, revive, enliven, liberate, make confident, effectual, etc. (as in "Brave Achilles *empowered* Patroclus by giving him his shield." "Jesus *empowered* Lazarus by raising him from the dead." "Harry *empowered* Glenda by giving her the checkbook." "A kiss *empowered* Sleeping Beauty, who had been *disempowered* by a spell.") Employment, authority, tolerance, psychoanalysis, religion, a Ph.D., pethidine, and nuclear weapons are all said to *empower* people. To validate, approve, justify, a wink and a nod, condone, suck, dog whistle, etc. (as in bigotry, prejudice, greed, malpractice, theft, etc.).

EXERCISE: Rewrite the following sentence as if you had never heard of *empowerment*:
"Hamlet had an issue in terms of *empowering* himself."

Enhance/enhanced/enhancing/enhancement: Improve, increase, grow, swell, enlarge, streamline, beautify, strengthen, etc. Make more efficient or effective; brighter, weightier, lighter, pointier, hairier, longer, thicker, etc. (as in "Our marriage was *enhanced* when Bob started on the amitriptyline, but then his prostate got *enhanced*"). Make more lifelike, more graphic, or more fun (as in sex or violence). The list is as long as human desire, aspiration, talent, etc., as deep as the oceans, etc., as rich as nature and experience, etc.

EXERCISE: Rewrite the following sentence without "enhancement":

"His untimely death was a tragedy in terms of his own life but an *enhancement* in terms of his status as an icon."

Event: Occurrence; something that happens, takes place, occurs, eventuates, etc., planned or unplanned. Planned events include concerts, sports meetings, rodeos, bullfights, poetry readings, boxing matches, tractor pulls, dances, etc. As these are sometimes known as sporting events, literary events, social events, musical events, etc., unplanned events such as earthquakes, storms, and car accidents are today likely to be called, respectively, geological *events,* severe weather *events,* and road trauma *events* ("The department has been informed that one or both of the dams partially failed during a recent rain *event*."—Michigan Department of Environmental Quality). In Australia a bushfire is now a "wildfire *event*" ("Come on, baby, light my fire *event*.") The space shuttle *Columbia* produced debris *events* as it disintegrated over the United States—the largest of them was called Debris Event 14; beavers are also responsible for debris *events* in American streams. "Taxable *events*" are "*events* with a tax consequence." That business has caught on to *events* is confirmed by the emergence of strategies to deal with them (as in "Strategies for responding to hiring *events*").

EXERCISE: Is there another way of putting this?
"And God said, Let there be a light *event*: and there was a light *event*."

Fora: (archaic plural of *forum*, revived for no apparent reason in the 1980s; sometimes made plural as *foras*) Forums (as in "various international *fora*"); meetings, conventions, gatherings, conferences; organizations, bodies, groups; parliaments, guilds, associations, clubs, etc.

EXERCISE: Rewrite the following sentence without using "fora:"
"Crossing Australia, the explorers Burke and Wills saw a lot of flora and *fora*."

Going forward: In future, the future, trajectory, not regressing or stalled, going on (*ongoing*); what generally happens without anyone needing to say so (as in "We have a strategy for continuous improvement outcomes *going forward*").

EXERCISE: Insert *going forward* into this sentence:
"And God said, Let there be light: and there was light."

Hopefully: With hope. Full of hope. With luck. With a bit of luck. I/we/they, etc., hope. If we're lucky. God willing. With every confident expectation. Here's hoping. With hope in our hearts. Here's looking up your kilt. Barring accident. Hope, hoping, hopeful (as in "I hope you are well." "Hoping to hear from you soon." "I am hopeful"). Also wish, desire, expect, anticipate, etc.

EXERCISE: Rewrite the following sentence with "hopefully" nowhere to be seen:

> "*Hopefully,* her faith was well founded and at the end of the day there is life after death."

Impact: (*v.* also *n.*, becoming rarer) To run, crash, thump, bang, etc. into (as in "We don't know how the drought will *impact* on farmers' bottom lines"). Affect, change, alter, shift, reshape, etc., the economy, the landscape, the airline industry, the status of women, football, the national identity, one's personal identity, one's hair, etc. Remake, transmogrify, transform, surprise, spruce up, let down, etc.

EXERCISE: Open your favorite Stephen King novel and substitute "impact" for the first seventeen verbs. Read aloud.

Implement: Do, realize, make happen, institute, put in train, create, give expression or effect to (as in "This offer is all part of our strategy of continuous improvement we are committed to *implementing*").

EXERCISE: Implement this in the original:
"And God said unto Noah . . . *implement* thee an ark of gopher wood . . . And Noah *implemented* three sons, Shem, Ham and Japheth."

Input: (*n.* and *v.*) Contribution, offering, assistance, help, advice, say, suggestion, something put in (as in "I would like to thank Gerard for his robust *input* tonight" or "If I may *input* a suggestion at this point in time").

EXERCISE: What is wrong with this sentence?
"Great and manifold were the *inputs,* most dread Sovereign, which Almighty God, the Father of all mercies, bestowed upon the people of England. . . ."

In terms of: In relation to, in regard to, in respect to; because, for (as in "I support it *in terms of* the benefits it will bring"); insofar, to the extent that; toward, to, about (as in "My attitude *in terms of* the prime minister is that he is lying *in terms of* the issue"); on (as in "France is likely to exert a lot of influence *in terms of* the final outcome").

EXERCISE: Rewrite the following sentence without "in terms of."
"Victoria reigned for more than sixty years and set a new benchmark *in terms of* being a queen."

Issue: That (anything) which you or your company has with another individual or company. The important matter or question to be resolved. Where the weight is. Also any problem, argument, complaint, difficulty, wound, sore spot, bone of contention, bone to pick, difference of opinion or belief, etc. (as in "I don't have an *issue* with you or Golden Crumpets, Ltd., Jeremy, but I think you might have an *issue* with me"). Whatever is going on between people, including rivalry, envy, lust (including financial lust), nonpayment of debts, lack of empowerment, lack of commitment, etc. *Issues* are core and non-core, key and non-key. Some people have health issues (as in "Those beans gave me digestive issues.")

EXERCISE: What *was* the issue with Hamlet?

"To be, or not to be—that is the *issue*."

Key: (cf. **core**) A thing with which to open something, especially a door or window; the reason for success; to type something in (*v.*); core (*adj.*) (as in "*key* promise," "*key* initiative," "*key* decision," "*key* strategy," "*key* commitment," etc.); the central, most efficacious, most demanding thing; crucial, decisive, essential, fundamental, most important, the best, cleverest, the one we want to stress, spend the most money on, etc.

EXERCISE: Rewrite the following sentence without using "key" (or "core").

"The leader of the expedition took a *key* initiative, and committed himself to no more than one bottle a day."

Market/marketing: Inform, encourage, persuade, sell, soft-soap, flog, media management/relations, manipulate, harass, spin, exaggerate, distort, bribe, blackmail, lure, frighten, deceive, lie, etc. (as in "There is nothing so vile that it can't be *marketed*").

EXERCISE: Think of something better to say than this:
"Whatever other issues you might have with Goebbels, he had a genius for *marketing*."

Outcome: Result, consequence, end, upshot, effect, conclusion, product, etc. What comes out of strategizing; hence, triumph, victory, good show, etc. Disaster, calamity, fizzer, net-negative, down the gurgler, not worth a crumpet, excellent—not, I don't think so, etc.

EXERCISE: Rewrite the following sentence without "outcome" (and other offending words):
"Gordon died at Khartoum, but hopefully he would not have been too disappointed in terms of the final *outcome*."

Point in time: Now, then, before, later, presently, earlier, in August, at 12:15 P.M. (as in "I didn't know at that *point in time* and I don't know at this *point in time*").

EXERCISE: Correct these sentences:
1. "Excuse me, can you tell me the *point in time*?"
2. "At that *point in time* was the Word."

Prioritize: To give precedence to. To put or do first. To attend to a task in preference to another. Rate above others.

Above all. Rank according to importance, urgency, affection, etc. (as in "I'm sorry, Thelma, but I've *prioritized* Jennifer in terms of my desire"). To judge foremost, paramount, preeminent, principal, main, essential, vital, the thing that matters now.

EXERCISE: Rewrite the following sentence without using "prioritize":

"At the end of the day Edward had to *prioritize* his commitments."

Product: Something that is produced, manufactured, grown, devised, invented, concocted, bequeathed, etc. Goods, chattels, potatoes, ideas, concepts, socks, secret intelligence, tourist promotions, education, books, plays and paintings, weather forecasts, greyhound races. Anything (as in "In fact, South Wales is coming up with a lot of new *product* in terms of tourism").

EXERCISE: Correct this sentence:

"There is more *product* in heaven and earth, Horatio,/ Than is dreamed of in your philosophy."

Robust: Strong, hardy, full of health and vigor, full-bodied, hearty. Until now applied in the main to people, animals, and wines; today strategies, plans, commitments, workshops, dialogues, debates, reforms, chicken recipes, cuisine, relationships, consumption, sales, monitoring systems, computer software, business practices, appetites including sexual appetites, business processes, business plans, markets, economies, software, and curriculum frameworks are declared *robust* or it is said that they should be (as in "The community wants a *robust* curriculum framework that reflects expectations about meeting young people's needs"). Much that was recently *vibrant* is now *robust*. Even scenarios are called *robust*. The challenge of being a customer-centric organization is confronted *robustly*. Armies take *robust* action against insurgents. The Americans make a Robust Multi-Pronged Food Thermometer, and they are planning to make a Robust Earth Penetrator High-Yield Weapon.

EXERCISE: Why didn't Churchill say this?
"Let us therefore brace ourselves to our duty, and so bear ourselves that, if the British Empire and its Commonwealth lasts for a thousand years, men will still say, 'This was their most *robust* hour.' "

Scenario: Summary, outline, or précis of a dramatic work or hypothetical or future events. Summary, outline, or précis of past and present events. Any events real, projected, or fancied. Any circumstances, projected or fancied (as in "It is not possible to give you a pay raise in the present *scenario,* Kylie, but in some future *scenario* it might be going forward").

EXERCISE: What's wrong with the following sentence?
"To be, or not to be—they are the *scenarios.*"

Strategic/strategically/strategize/strategizing/strategy: Clever, smart, farsighted, very clever (as in a *strategic* plan, policy campaign, etc.). Anything better than stupid, misguided, wrong, etc. Well planned, well husbanded, well marshalled. Tactical, considered, measured, etc. Antonyms: nonstrategic, unstrategic, myopic, playing it by ear, ad hoc, flexible, adaptable, free, light on one's feet, exceedingly clever.

EXERCISE: Rewrite the following sentence without using "strategy":

> "Scott of the Antarctic was brave and hardy and deserves his status as an icon, but at the end of the day he lacked an exit *strategy*."

Text: Printed words; a book; the contents of a book or other printed work; the exact words; a printed work for discussion or study (as in "I can read you like a *text*"). Anything for discussion or study. Anything written, spoken, filmed, painted, or expressed, recorded, or rendered in some way. Anything *authored* (as in "Would that mine adversary had written a *text*"). Anything that appears to exist. *King Lear, Fawlty Towers, Silas Marner,* Donald Duck, "Things go better with Coke," etc. Hence *textish* or *textworm*—one who reads many texts. (*v.*) Send an SMS message.

EXERCISE: What does "text" mean in the context of this *text*?

> "Your face, my thane, is as a *text* where men
> May read strange matters."

Workshop: (*n.*) A place of work. A meeting for the purpose of discussion, debate, role playing, self-actualization, large group awareness training, identification and targeting of

key goals, values, etc.; organizational alignment of
processes, inputs, outputs, outcomes going forward, etc.
(as in "We spent the whole weekend at a *workshop* on deliverables"). (*v.*) To do any of the foregoing, often with a
consultant, in a rural or seaside environment. To talk in a
structured environment with the aid of a facilitator; to di-
alogue, brainstorm, enter the matrix, talk the talk (in
preparation for walking it), to self-enhance, to bond with
the team, to waste one's life, etc. (cf. "If there's one word
that sums up everything that's gone wrong since the war,
it's *workshop*."—Kingsley Amis, *Jake's Thing*).

EXERCISE: On a scale of one to ten, rate the following
assertions:

"I *workshop,* therefore I am."

"What a piece of *workshopping* is a man."

"If any would not *workshop,* neither should he eat."

ACKNOWLEDGMENTS

•

Most of the material for this book has been drawn from my own experience as a speechwriter, as a customer, a taxpayer, a voter, a reader of newspapers, an observer of sports, a frequenter of streets, a victim of television and the Internet, a citizen. What I did not glean myself, other people sent me, mainly from the places where they work. In this way they added to the quality and variety of my exhibits and at the same time assured me that I was not a crank.

In the last few years I have met hundreds of people who share my concern. They have been teachers and students, public and private employees, people with telephones, bank accounts, and insurance policies, customers, consumers—all kinds of people. I thank all of them for helping me, or being, as they say everywhere these days, so supportive.

My wife, Hilary McPhee, was not only supportive; the book was her idea. For that and much else I thank her once again. Jane Palfreyman was very supportive too; in fact, as a publisher she is the benchmark in terms of supportiveness. Rose Creswell was also supportive, and I thank her as well, along with Murray Bail for his usual stimulation. Helen Smith was supportive in a core way. I thank Karen Pryor for a couple of gems and Nadine Davidoff. Also Bruce Petty for honoring me with his endpapers.

And Sandy Hollway, who, years ago, when everyone else seemed content with the existing scenario, agreed that there was something rotten in the public language, and faxed an example from the Department of Finance that has been an inspiration and a keepsake ever since.

> Given the within year and budget time flexibility ac-
> corded to the science agencies in the determination of re-
> source allocation from within their global budget, a
> multi-parameter approach to maintaining the agencies
> budgets in real terms is not appropriate.

This is a true, possibly world-class, death sentence, and I am pleased to give it a home at last.

BIBLIOGRAPHY

•

Peter F. Alexander, *Les Murray: A Life in Progress* (Oxford University Press, 2000).

Martin Amis, *The War Against Cliché* (Vintage, 2002).

Don Anderson, "Angel of Devastation" in *Text and Sex* (Vintage, 1995).

W. H. Auden, *Collected Shorter Poems 1930–1934* (Faber and Faber, 1944).

Francis Bacon, *Essays* (J. M. Dent, 1999).

Bill Bryson, *Mother Tongue* (Penguin, 1991).

Robert Burchfield, *The English Language* (Oxford University Press, 1985).

Italo Calvino, *Hermit in Paris* (Jonathan Cape, 2003).

Jean-Claude Carrière, *The Secret Language of Film* (Faber and Faber, 1995).

Walter de la Mare, *Stories from the Bible* (Faber and Faber, n.d.).

Joan Didion, "Fixed Opinions, or The Hinge of History," *New York Review of Books* (January 16, 2003).

Joan Didion, *Political Fictions* (Knopf, 2001).

T. S. Eliot, "The Hippopotamus," *Collected Poems 1909–1935* (Faber and Faber, 1951).

William Faulkner, *As I Lay Dying* (Vintage, 1996).

Gustave Flaubert, *Dictionary of Received Ideas* (Penguin, 1976).

Eduardo de la Fuente, "Where Is Politics at the End of History?" *Arena* (February/March 1996).

Ulysses S. Grant, *Personal Memoirs* (Penguin, 1999).

Homer, *The Odyssey*, tr. Robert Fagles (Penguin, 1997).

Elmore Leonard, *Be Cool* (Penguin, 1999).

Primo Levi, *Other People's Trades* (Simon & Schuster, 1989).

Norman Mailer, *The Armies of the Night* (Signet, 1968).

David Marr and Marion Wilkinson, *Dark Victory* (Allen and Unwin, 2003).

Czeslaw Milosz, *Native Realm: A Search for Self-Definition* (Farrar, Strauss, & Giroux, 2002).

Robert T. Oliver, *The Influence of Rhetoric in the Shaping of Great Britain* (Associated University Presses, 1986).

George Orwell, *Animal Farm* (Longmans, 1962).

George Orwell, "Politics and the English Language," *Inside the Whale and Other Essays* (Penguin, 1962).

Christopher Ricks and Leonard Michaels (eds.), *The State of the Language* (University of California Press, 1990).

Philip Roth, quoted in the *Daily Telegraph* (October 5, 2002).

William Safire, *Lend Me Your Ears: Great Speeches in History* (Norton, 1997).

Earl Shorris, "The Last Word" *Harpers* (August 2000).

Russell Smith, "The New Newspeak," *New York Review of Books* (May 29, 2003).

William Strunk Jr. and E. B. White, *The Elements of Style,* 3rd edition (Macmillan, 1979).

Rob Watts, "Down and Out . . ." *Journal of Institutional Research* (October–November 2003).

Simone Weil, "*The Iliad*, Poem of Force" 1940–41 (Peter Lang Publishing, 2003).

Garry Wills, *Lincoln at Gettysburg* (Simon & Schuster, 1992).

Keith Windshuttle and Elizabeth Elliott, *Writing, Researching and Communicating* (Irwin/McGraw Hill, 2002).

W. B. Yeats, "The Lake Isle of Innisfree," "An Irish Airman Foresees His Death," *Collected Poems* (Macmillan, 1955).